E. A. Waldron

The Sea Coast Resorts

of Eastern Maine, New Brunswick, Nova Scotia

E. A. Waldron

The Sea Coast Resorts
of Eastern Maine, New Brunswick, Nova Scotia

ISBN/EAN: 9783743394957

Manufactured in Europe, USA, Canada, Australia, Japa

Cover: Foto ©Andreas Hilbeck / pixelio.de

Manufactured and distributed by brebook publishing software (www.brebook.com)

E. A. Waldron

The Sea Coast Resorts

THE
Sea Coast Resorts

—:OF:—

Eastern Maine, New Brunswick, Nova Scotia, Prince Edward Island, and Cape Breton.

PUBLISHED BY THE
INTERNATIONAL STEAMSHIP COMPANY.

Tickets and General Information may be obtained at the following Agencies of the Company:—

E. A. WALDRON GENERAL AGENT, COMMERCIAL WHARF, BOSTON.

Local Agents.

Boston, Mass................................CHAS. F. CONN, City Ticket Agent, 207 Washington Street.
Portland, Me................................H. P. C. HERSEY, Railroad Wharf.
Eastport, Me................................A. H. LEAVITT, International S. S. Company's Wharf.
Calais, Me..................................JAS. L. THOMPSON, Frontier Steamboat Company.
St. John, N.B...............................C. E. LAECHLER, Reed's Point Wharf.

Tickets can be obtained at offices of Southern and Western Lines; the Fall River, Providence, Stonington and Norwich lines of steamers; also in New England and the Provinces.

J. B. COYLE, *Manager,*   E. A. WALDRON, *General Agent,*
    PORTLAND, ME.   BOSTON, MASS.

C. H. SANBORN, *General Travelling Agent,* BOSTON, MASS.

STEAMER STATE OF MAINE.

DISTANCES AND TIME.

	MILES	TIME
BOSTON TO PORTLAND...............	110	7½ hours.
BOSTON TO EASTPORT (direct), about......	260	30 "
PORTLAND TO EASTPORT	190	14 "
EASTPORT TO ST. JOHN...........	58	3½ "
EASTPORT TO CALAIS	30	2½ "
EASTPORT TO ST. ANDREWS	18	1½ "
ST. JOHN TO HALIFAX (Rail)...........	276	10 "
ST. JOHN TO HALIFAX (Water and Rail)...	190	12 "

DISTAN[CES]

ST. JOHN TO SUMMERSI[DE]
ST. JOHN TO CHARLOTTE[TOWN]
ST. JOHN TO FREDERICT[ON]
ST. JOHN TO DIGBY.....
ST. JOHN TO ANNAPOLIS
ST. JOHN TO YARMOUTH
ST. JOHN TO STRAIT [OF]

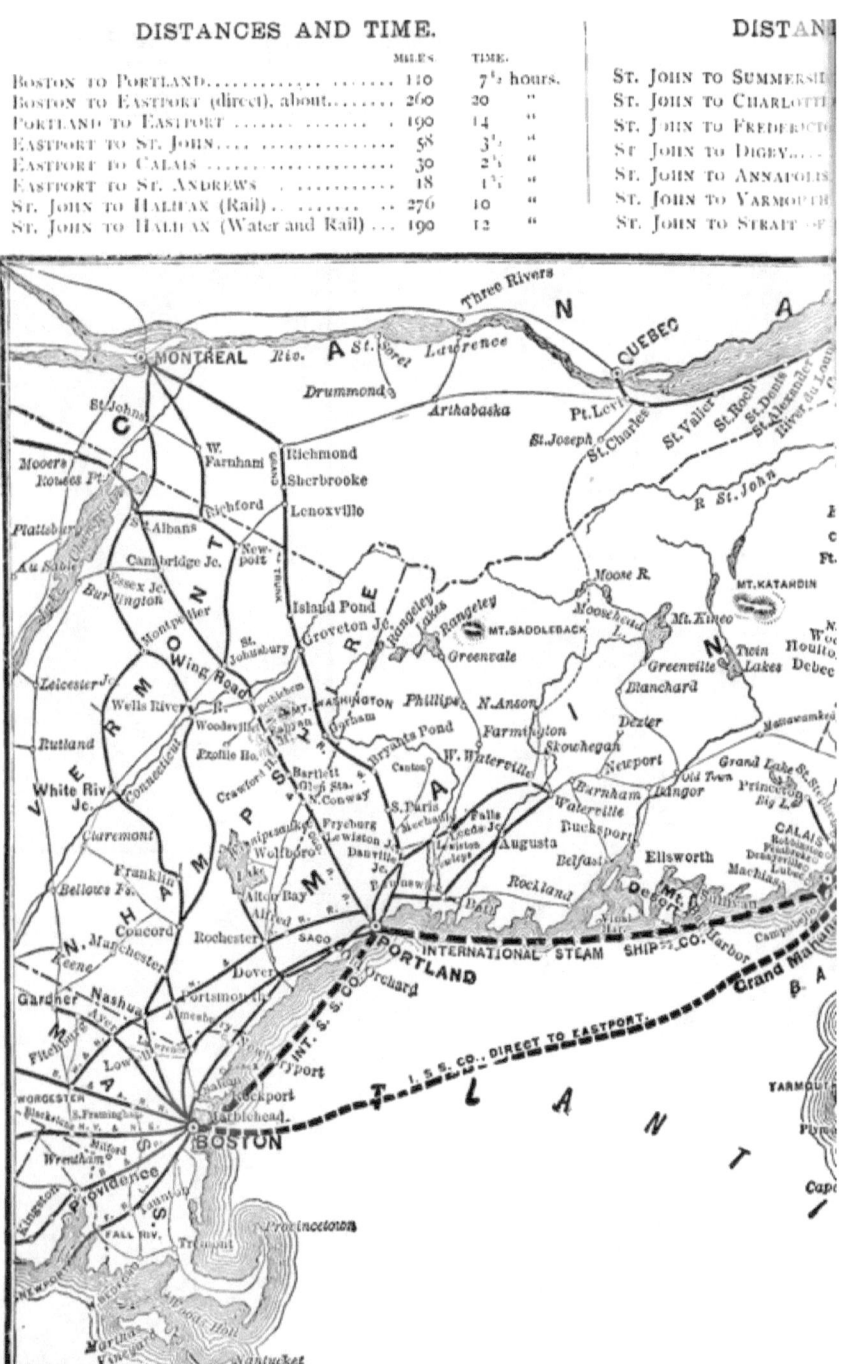

D TIME.

MILES.	TIME.	
...... 167	9	hours.
.1..... 216	12	"
:er)..... 80	9	"
...... 45	3½	"
...... 60	4½	"
...... 112	10	"
...... 338	16	"

THROUGH TICKETS
AND BAGGAGE CHECKED TO AND FROM PHILADELPHIA, BALTIMORE AND WASHINGTON.

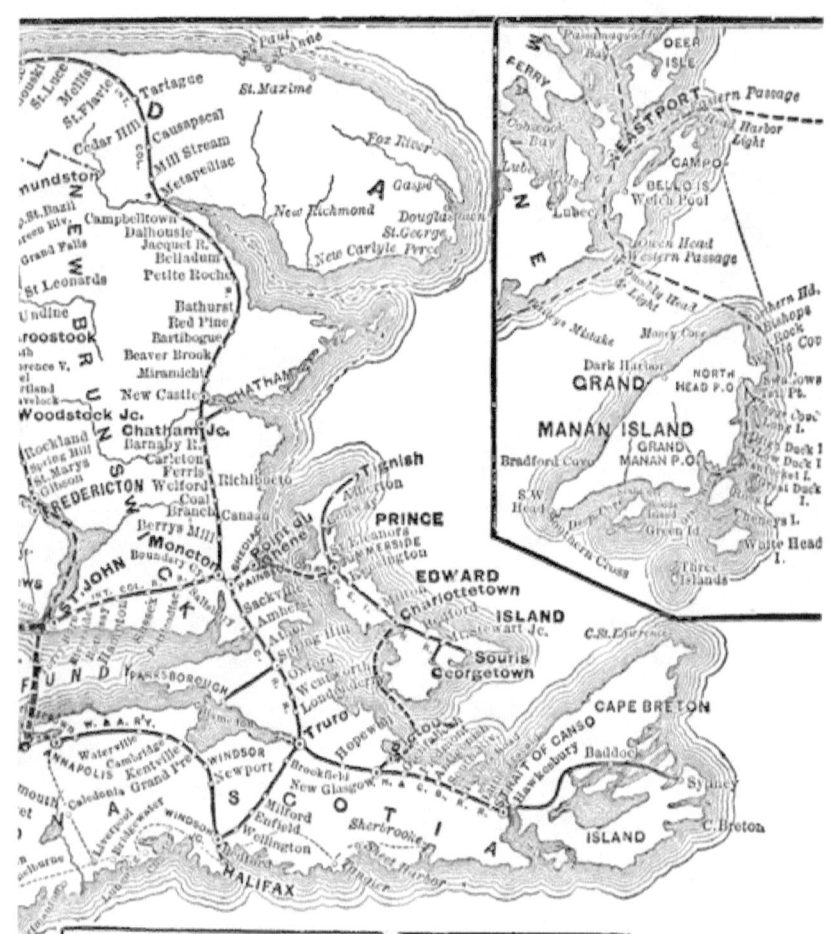

MAP SHOWING THE
INTERNATIONAL STEAMSHIP CO.'S
ROUTES

STEAMER CUMBERLAND.

PREFACE.

Recognizing the fact that the space afforded in this book will not permit a liberal description of the summer resorts reached by the International Steamship Company and its connections, the writer has endeavored to portray the route from its western to eastern limit, giving the attractions of the water-journey together with an abridged pen-picture of the scenes encountered by the voyager in eastern seas, from the port of Boston to and beyond the United States boundary.

This, then, is presented with the hope that whatever is lacking of interest and beauty may be discovered by the tourist in person, and that the daylight ocean voyage may not be forgotten in planning the holiday trip.

E. A. WALDRON,
General Agent,
International S. S. Co.

TABLE OF CONTENTS.

	PAGE
PREFACE	2
CHAPTER I. — The Invitation, introducing the Old North-East — The International Steamship Line — Its Tourist Facilities — Its Ships	5
CHAPTER II. — The St. John Route in Detail — Boston the Starting Point — Boston Harbor and Massachusetts Bay — Eastward, Ho! — The Isles of Shoals — Boon Island — Saline Types — Old Orchard and Connecting Beaches — The Grand View of the White Mountains — The Harbor Lights of Portland	8
CHAPTER III. — Portland, Maine — Entrance to its Harbor, the Cape Shore and Islands — A War-time Incident — Through the City — Longfellow — The Union Station — Train Facilities — A Bit Historical	13
CHAPTER IV. — Eastward from Portland — Casco Bay — Harpswell — Halfway Rock — Seguin, the Mouth of the Kennebec — Monhegan — Pemaquid — The Sea-fight Far Away	19
CHAPTER V. — Passamaquoddy, and About There — Phenomenal Tides — As a Health Resort — General Greeley's Testimony — A Passamaquoddy Incident — Eastport — North Lubec — Cutler — Pembroke — Perry — Dennysville — Robbinston — Campobello — Grand Manan — St. Andrews	23
CHAPTER VI. — The St. Croix River — The Schoodic Lakes — Sporting Possibilities — The Ascent of the River — Douchet's Island — The Des Monts Expedition — The Magaguadavic River and Lake Eutopia — Calais and St. Stephen — The Rule of the Road	37
CHAPTER VII. — From Eastport to St. John — Bay of Fundy Glimpses — St. John — Points of Interest — The " Reversible Cataract" — Historical Pictures — The River St. John — Its Fishing and Hunting Possibilities — The New Brunswick Railway	45
CHAPTER VIII. — New Brunswick for Sport — The Salmon Streams, How to Reach Them — The Miramichi — The Tobique — Headwaters of the St. John — Grand Falls	55
CHAPTER IX. — The Northern Province — Intercolonial Railway — Some of its Towns — Its Fishing Resorts — Grand Falls of the Nepisiquit — Restigouche and Metapedia — Lake and River — Provincial Game Laws, and Close Time	58
CHAPTER X. — Prince Edward Island and Cape Breton — The Garden of Nova Scotia — The Passage of the Ice-boats — Summerside, Charlottetown — A Cheap Bill of Fare — The Round-about Route — Cape Breton Island — Bras D'Or — The Arm of Gold — Geological Wonders — Coal Deposits — The Marble Mountain — Louisburg — An Historical Revel	67
CHAPTER XI. — The Lower Peninsula of Nova Scotia — Halifax, the Metropolis of the Province — The Rail Route to the Annapolis Valley	77
CHAPTER XII. — St. John to Digby, Annapolis, and the Land of Evangeline — Annapolis Royal — Grand Pré — The Story of the Acadians — Grande Finale	81

LIST OF ILLUSTRATIONS.

Cape Elizabeth and Portland Head	7
City of Portland	14
White Head and Portland Observatory	17
Bits of Casco Bay and the Maine Coast	18
Friar's Head and Lubec	23
Around Eastport	26
Campobello Bits	30
Whale Cove, Grand Manan	32
Grand Manan Pictures	34
St. Andrews	35
Passamaquoddy Bay and the St. Croix	36
Lake Utopia and the Falls of St. George	40
Passamaquoddy Fishing Boats	43
Mt. Desert Hills	44
In St. John Harbor	46
On St. John River	48
Near Fredericton, N.B.	53
Head Harbor, Campobello, N.B.	54
On the Restigouche	60
Lake Metapedia	62
Frazer's Head on Minas Basin	64
Pastoral Scene, P. E. Island	66
A Vacation Day	68
Strait of Canso from Hawkesbury	71
Cliffs near Grand Narrows, C.B.	74
Sydney and the Falls near Baddeck	75
Point Lepreaux Light	76
Cape Split, from Baxter's Harbor	79
Partridge Island	80
Petit Manan Light	83
In Grand Pré Village	87
West Quoddy Light	88
View from International Steamship Co.'s Dock, Eastport	93
St. Andrews and Vicinity	96

CHAPTER FIRST

INTRODUCTORY TO THE REGION REACHED BY THE INTERNATIONAL STEAMSHIP LINE — THE COMPANY'S SHIPS AND SERVICE.

> "There is a society where none intrude,
> By the deep sea; and music in its roar."

AN OCEAN VOYAGE in connection with my summer's outing? Yes! An ocean voyage, in palatial steamers, thoroughly staunch and of sea-going qualities as complete as are their fine appointments and *cuisine*.

But first tell me whither will your fancy lead? Shall it be to the eastward, to the numerous health and pleasure resorts along the coast or in the interior of the State of Maine; or farther still beyond the International boundary, where lies a vast country under British dominion, full of beauty and crowned with a wealth of interest, replete with the blended romance, story and tradition connected with the earliest settlement of the North American continent?

A country which gave refuge to the early voyagers from Europe, at a time when the Pilgrim Fathers of the Old Colony were in leading strings, and now through two centuries presents its peculiar manners, customs and civilization as an auxiliary charm to the summer tourist from "The States," giving him a taste of Europe only to be found this side the Atlantic; in this quaint Old North-East, this country under the shadow of the Crown, this "Land of Evangeline" and the British Red-coat. Novelty adds to the pleasures of the outing, for

> 'Tis by novelty enjoyment lives.

Therefore, in planning the itinerary for your summer tour, ye pilgrims from the heat and dust of cities, bear in mind the water routes offered by the INTERNATIONAL STEAMSHIP COMPANY, and follow its pathways through Maine-coast waves to the eastern country, or make one of its terminals the gateway for reaching your chosen goal.

The best part of going to sea is keeping near the shore, which presents an ever-changing panorama to the view. This is one of the charms of the International Line. Its steamers, running within sight of the coast line, introduce its patrons to the many interesting points along shore ; a sort of voyage of discovery which includes city, town, village and country ; the physical features, capes, bays and promontories, rugged barriers of the sea, and last, but not least, the tall beacons which light the shoals and harbors.

There is nothing which inspires the mind of man like the lighthouse, which, crowning the rocky headlands along shores, flash their warnings one to another and far to sea, thus by their peculiarity of light forming a sort of flash and darkness system of telegraphy, which tells the sailor not only of the approach to land, but his position also.

> "I lit the lamps in the lighthouse tower,
>   For the sun dropped down and the day was dead ;
> They shone like a golden clustered flower —
>   Two golden and five red."

John Quincy Adams says, he never saw these coast-lights in the evening without recalling to mind the light Columbus saw flashing from shore the night he discovered the New World.

If there is inspiration to be drawn from them it must occur in the passage of the International Steamers on the ocean-voyage from Boston Light to Quoddy Head, and farther within the Bay of Fundy, with the lights along the North Shore of Massachusetts Bay, Cape Ann, Thatcher's Island, Isle of Shoals, Boon Island, Cape Elizabeth, Portland Head, Half-Way Rock, Seguin, Monhegan, Pemaquid Point, and a host of others intervening.

In connection with its steamship lines this company has established a complete system of tourist routes and rates (see pages 90–95), covering all rail and steamboat lines necessary for reaching the summer-resorts of Maine, and the White Mountains of New Hampshire, as well as those within the Maritime Provinces of New Brunswick and Nova Scotia.

Prince Edward Island and Cape Breton, while the new and growing popular resort of Cutler (Maine), Famous Grand Manan, the charming Passamaquoddy Bay, resting retreats of Campobello Island and St. Andrews-by-the-sea, are reached best by its own line, which continuing on to St. John (New Brunswick), and by connecting steamer across the Bay of Fundy to the quaint towns of Digby and Annapolis (Nova Scotia), in the "Annapolis Basin," finds there the gateway through which the traveller reaches all Provincial points.

The Company, founded in 1860, has at the present time in commission three of the finest steamers in eastern waters, — the "State of Maine," "Cumberland," and the "New Brunswick." The two former are Bath-built side-wheel craft of 1,600 tons burden, constructed during the years 1882 and 1885 respectively, by the ship-building company, modern in every particular, and rival the floating palaces of Long Island Sound. No expense is spared by the liberal management of the line in keeping its steamers up to a high standard of excellency. The *menu* and table service is unsurpassed.

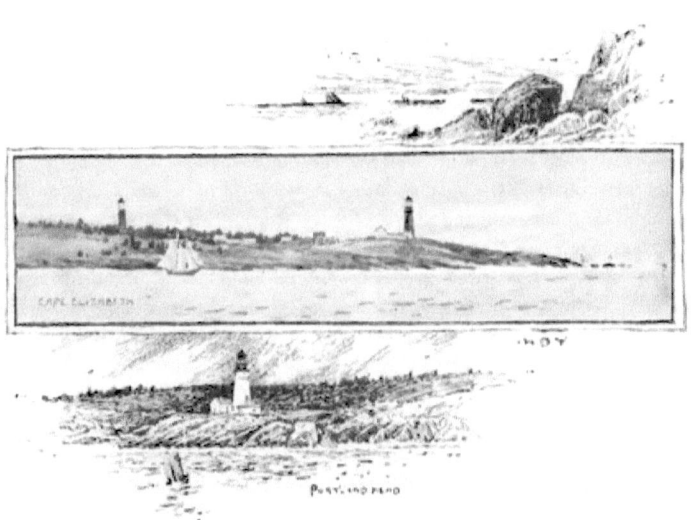

CHAPTER SECOND

THE ST. JOHN ROUTE IN DETAIL.—SIGHTS ALONG THE COAST FROM
BOSTON TO PORTLAND—THE ISLES OF SHOALS,
OLD ORCHARD BEACH, ETC.

BOSTON is the grand focal point to which converging lines from ALL AMERICA concentrate the throng of eastern tourist travel, each season growing larger as the manifold attractions which the country holds are advertised, and advertise themselves, as no pen can, to the health-seeking, pleasure-seeking summer visitor.

There are rail routes and water routes for again distributing this throng, but only one line, the International Steamship Company, offers the attraction of a "thro'-by-daylight" sail via Portland. This is a distinctive feature. Then, too, the sea voyage has ever been the panacea for human ills of the brain-wearied, *ennuied* order, so we will fancy the tourist — for the outing is to be a search for combined health and pleasure — embarked upon one of the good ships of the line, for the voyage, Eastward, Ho! The route skirts the coast for a great part of the distance, so there is little fear of *mal-de-mer*.

All in good time the steamer bears away, at an hour when the harbor scene is brightest, and the points of interest are clearly in view, past Fort Independence, with Deer Island, on which are the city institutions of charity and the house of correction, and the main land of Winthrop upon the left. The seventy-five islands and islets which exist within the encircling arms of the three — Dorchester, Quincy and Hingham bays, which constitute the harbor of "The Hub"— are clustered in the seaward landscape.

Looking toward the city the united Charles and Mystic rivers are seen entering the sea, dividing East Boston from the city proper; while in line with the former rises Bunker Hill Monument above the heights of Charlestown.

From the city of Boston to the final point of egress from its harbor, the outlet of the main ship channel, the distance is about seven miles. The passage is filled with interest throughout. After leaving the harbor the ship's course is shaped along the north shore of Massachusetts Bay, with the tall white beacons, discernible from the decks, standing singly and in doubles so plentifully along this coast, where at night their signal fires blaze far across the waters like fallen stars from Heaven, guiding the sailor to the hospitable harbors of Swampscott, Marblehead, Salem, Gloucester, and a hundred lesser ports, a succession of attractive seacoast cities and towns, loaded with interest, song and story.

> "You may ride in an hour or two if you will,
> From Halibut Point to Beacon Hill,
> With the sea beside you all the way.
> Through pleasant places that skirt the Bay;
> By Gloucester Harbor and Beverly Beach,
> Salem's old steeples, Nahant's long reach,
> Blue-bordered Swampscott, and Chelsea's wide
> Marshes, laid bare to the drenching tide,
> With a glimpse of Saugus spire in the west,
> And Malden hills in their dreamy rest."

Halibut Point is the extreme northern point on Cape Ann, Cape Ann the extreme limit of Massachusetts Bay, Beacon Hill the acme of the exclusive exclusiveness of the city of Boston.

The above lines from the pen of Lucy Larcom fitly describe the route of the steamer from the wharves of Boston to the limit of Cape Ann, for as straight as the chart directs, the course of the steamer has been for Thatcher's Island, lying off the eastern point of the cape, midway between the ports of Gloucester and Rockport, and proudly bearing the cape lights.

At the entrance to the harbor of Gloucester, where is now a summer settlement bearing the name Magnolia, lies the luckless reef of Norman's Woe, famous as the scene of Longfellow's poem, "Wreck of the Hesperus." Leaving Thatcher's Island the steamer heads direct for its next objective point, the harbor lights of Portland, Maine.

Now the curving coast line of New Hampshire and of Maine permits the ocean voyage; and between the two points, for a few hours only, the steamer passes "out of sight of land." The cruise outside between Cape Ann and Portland is varied by the approach and passage of the Isles of Shoals, with their color of romance. These islands, a half dozen in number, lie in two States, their position directly off the mouth of the Piscataqua River, which forms the boundary between New Hampshire and Maine, and about nine miles from the coast; from their position there arose a question of jurisdiction, growing out of a most atrocious murder committed on Smutty Nose during the year 1873. The murderer was finally tried in the Maine courts, and suffered for his crime at Thomaston, the site of the Maine State Prison. Other startling crimes have colored the history of the Isles of Shoals. No section of country could contribute a larger or more thrilling volume in the records of piracy in the New World than these islands. It is certain that in the olden time they formed the rendezvous of such noted buccaneers as Kidd, Dixey Bull and Blackbeard.

This was a desirable place to refit or repair ships. Troublesome questions and questionable appearances were avoided, as the pirate craft lay sheltered in the roads between these high headlands, while their crews found shelter amid the rocky fortresses ashore. To relate the tales of wreck and ruin wrought by the pirate kings who have cruised to the Isles of Shoals to bury their ill-gotten treasure among the rocks, or the recital of the fearful sights and sounds which have met those whose hardihood permitted the search for the hidden wealth, would fill a volume and satisfy the most hungry sensationalist of the times.

Star Island, one of New Hampshire's possessions, bears a monument erected in 1864 to the memory of Captain John Smith of early colonial fame, and White Island bears the warning light of the Shoals.

Boon Island, a lonely, desolate rock with a tall beacon, lies some distance east of the Isles of Shoals, directly off the coast of Maine, some twelve miles distant from the historic town of York. As we pass it to-day one can scarcely credit the story of the wreck of the Nottingham and the terrible scenes of cannibalism among her crew, who were held prisoners by the waves upon the wild rock during twenty-four days in December, 1811. Wonder not then at the number of the coast lights which warn the sailors of to-day against a fate so dire.

But now a bountiful dinner is being served within the spacious saloon, at which there is always a merry company, and after which there is time for a delightful siesta upon the promenade deck, in easy steamer chairs, where, fanned by the salt breath of the sea, with book on lap, one may lazily pass the time, or curiously study the queer saline types of humanity to be met always in the passage of the Northern New England coast.

Engage such a one in conversation, and you are repaid by tales of the coast. He knows every bay and headland from Boston Light to Quoddy Head, and farther east to the "Grand Banks" of Newfoundland, of marvelous catches and prodigious bags of game; for your old salt is a born gunner, with sea-fowl his lawful prize. A life by the sea begets a spirit of sturdy independence, therefore he is a political economist of no mean order, indeed, the student of human nature can find no better field in which to pursue his studies than on the coast line of New England. Happily he will not be slow to discover the kindly side to the character of these quaint old salts.

Now the ship again approaches the coast and one sees the long line of Old Orchard Beach, with its mammoth hotels. Just west of Old Orchard's broad sweep, as may be plainly seen from the deck, the curving coast extends seaward to Biddeford Pool, at the mouth of the Saco River. Between this point and the "Two Lights" on Cape Elizabeth's shore extend in one continuous line numerous beaches which form the rallying-place for many summer guests.

They may be considered environments of Portland, being reached many times daily by a half-hour rail ride from the city, or by carriage ride over delightful shore roads beside the sounding sea. They are, in their order, Old Orchard, Pine Point, Scarborough and Higgins' Beaches, with Prout's Neck, a narrow peninsula, as its name implies, extending far into the bay at a point where the Nonesuch River and its estuary forms the only break in this great stretch of sand.

These form a succession of the grandest cooling-off places which Nature has provided for a long-suffering public. To one who delights in the ocean—and who does not?—they conjure up pleasant memories of gradually sloping beach of the whitest sea-sand, washed continually by giant breakers, among which sport a throng of bathers in every non-descript costume known to that gay pastime.

Two score hotels, large and small, line the beaches, facing seaward, where orchestras, hops and fashionable doings are the order of the day and night among three thousand guests.

It is while the steamer is passing this point that in a clear day the passengers are treated to the fairest view of the distant White Mountains of New Hampshire to be had from any equally distant point.

This view from the sea is particularly striking. There are other and nearer elevations which are ofttimes confounded with the White Mountains by strangers to this region, but the scene which these everlasting hills here present once seen is never forgotten nor miscalled.

Mt. Washington is ninety and odd miles distant in an air line from the city of Portland, yet the whole chain, of which Washington forms the highest and grandest elevation, stands out in individual distinction. They may be seen again at a point after leaving the city, but the view is incomparable to this.

After passing Old Orchard the twin beacons of the "Two Lights" upon the Cape Elizabeth shore come into view, then "Portland Head" light marking the entrance to the first harbor entered by the steamer in the daylight run from Boston. The noble headlands of this shore, bold, storm-defying, rugged types of Maine's rugged coast, have formed the subject of many a grand marine painting, and given inspiration to artist and poet.

> "Even at this distance I can see the tides,
> Upheaving, break unheard along the base;
> A speechless wrath that rises and subsides,
> In the white lip, and tremor of the face.
>
> "'Sail on!' it says, 'sail on' ye stately ships,
> And with your fleeting bridge the oceans span;
> Be mine to guard this light from all eclipse,
> Be yours to bring man nearer unto man.'"

A passing incident in connection with the "Two Lights" may here prove of interest. Just within their shadow, upon the rocks surrounding Broad Cove, Cape Elizabeth, the good ship Bohemian, an iron English mail steamer of the Allan Line, for whom Portland forms the winter port during the close time of the St. Lawrence River by ice, struck and was torn in pieces by the waves one stormy April morning of the year 1862.

Many lives were lost upon this *the last occasion of disaster to a passenger steamer, attended by loss of life, which has visited the eastern shore.*

Can many transportation lines, carrying the traffic which offers upon these favorite water routes, show a better record than thirty years without loss of life to its thousands carried yearly?

CHAPTER THIRD.

PORTLAND, MAINE, THE BIRTHPLACE OF LONGFELLOW — A PICTURESQUE
HARBOR AT SUNDOWN — THROUGH THE CITY —
ROUTES TO NOTED TOURIST RESORTS.

> "Often I think of the beautiful town
> That is seated by the sea;
> Often in thought go up and down
> The pleasant streets of that dear old town,
> And my youth comes back to me."

THE entrance to Portland harbor, after passing the light at Portland Head, is through the broad ship channel with the Cape Shore upon the left, and Cushing's Island forming the right extreme.

An extended view of Portland's summer hotels and cottages may be had from this point. The Cape Shore is lined with the summer homes of the city's business men, many of them most imposing subjects of modern architecture. This shore also bears pleasant hotels, the Cape Cottage and Ocean House for example, many boarding-houses, and the coast defences of the city whose sunset gun speeds the departing day.

Upon Cushing's, to the right, rises the broad roof and dome of "The Ottawa," the finest hotel in the harbor, new in 1889, to replace one destroyed the previous season. Beautiful cottages also adorn Cushing's, which is the most exclusive of Casco's isles.

Immediately after rounding the point of this island the city bursts upon the view from its commanding position upon the peninsula heights three miles distant.

The view from seaward in the approach to the city is incomparable, and is, indeed, the only point of view which shows Portland to advantage. The time of arrival at this point is most opportune for sight-seeing. The sun, yet well up in the heavens directly above the city, behind whose roofs and spires it sinks into the west with most charming cloud effects of ever-varying hue.

The harbor scene is most attractive, for the mammoth steamer is now in the path of the many excursion boats plying between the city and its cottage-covered suburban islands. Among them our ship seems colossal, and we are, for the passing moment, the centre of attraction to the gay groups who throng the decks of the smaller craft, which now are dancing

PORTLAND, ME.

in the huge swell of our wake. Thousands visit "The Islands" daily, a fleet of ten boats making constant trips; cottages and club-houses, innumerable almost, shelter the summer population, while the white tents of campers are anchored in every available spot.

Steam and sailing craft of every style are met or passed in the ascent of the harbor — a harbor which bears this distinction — let us turn from descriptive to incident, and relate it.

This busy harbor formed the theatre of action for the only invasion of a northern port by the enemy during the war of the rebellion; when the revenue cutter Caleb Cushing was "cut out" from under the guns of the now obsolete fort upon the right, by an armed force, who, at midnight — 1863 — overpowered her crew and succeeded in getting away with the craft, an armed sailing schooner of modest size.

No doubt the Cushing would have been turned into a privateer by her captors, had not her absence been discovered at daybreak from the observatory — mark the building, in form like the coast lights we have been passing — which crowns the eastern extremity of the city, and from which all vessels entering the port are signaled. Pursuit was made in two steamers, the Forest City and the Chesapeake. The latter, of the Portland-New York line, was herself afterward captured on the high sea by a band of confederates, who joined the ship in New York as passengers, took possession and sailed to an English port.

These two steamers pursued the cutter, overtook her becalmed about twenty miles from shore, where the cutting-out party, with the crew as prisoners, abandoned the ship after firing her magazine, blowing the trim little schooner into fragments.

Through the lively phases of the harbor scene the steamer makes its way along the complete water front of the city, with glimpses of the elm-shaded streets which have won for it the sobriquet of "The Forest City," to its berth at railroad wharf, foot of State Street.

It is but a short walk up this broad avenue, State Street, to the street-cars for "down town;" carriages also are awaiting the arrival. The cars pass all hotels, through the principal thoroughfares of retail trade, Congress and Middle Streets, to the wharves of the island steamers. Ignoring the street-cars yet for a few moments, however, a quarter mile walk through State Street straight from the steamer, one of the handsomest *old* avenues that the world affords, brings one to State Street Square, which contains a fine bronze statue of the poet Longfellow, the first erected in his honor, save the bust in Westminster Abbey.

We shall see much of Longfellow here at his birthplace and early home, and again in the voyage eastward to the country and people he has immortalized in that American classic, "Evangeline." Taking street-cars in this square a ride of five minutes' duration brings the traveller to the new and palatial Union Passenger Railway Station. This is the gateway to interior Maine, and the White Mountains, via the Maine Central Railroad, whose trains are replete with every convenience of travel, and each season bear a host of summer visitors to the hunting and fishing resorts of Rangeley and Moosehead lakes, and whose Mountain Division reaches the White Mountain resorts through the wonderland of the Crawford Notch.

Here it is possible to take a train with Pullman sleepers at eleven o'clock each night of the week, which shall bear the visitor to Bar Harbor and the many fashionable resorts on Mt. Desert Island in season for breakfast next morning. Here also numerous trains depart daily for Poland Spring, with its superb hotel, the eastern Ponce de Leon, as well as for all interior and coast towns of the State of Maine.

The "Union" is between the Maine Central and Boston and Maine railroads, who use together this beautiful and commodious station, to the mutual advantage of themselves and patrons. The Boston and Maine trains make frequent trips to the line of beaches which we saw from the steamer just beyond the Cape Shore, for Old Orchard direct, and for Scarboro Beach, Pine Point and Prout's Neck, from Scarboro and Pine Point stations, where carriage conveyance is in waiting for all beach hotels.

It is but twelve miles from the city of Portland to Old Orchard Beach, and the train delivers its passengers directly in the midst of one of the liveliest seashore scenes in the world. The beach is but a hundred yards distant, its great combing surf line making itself known at once. The largest hotels upon the coast of Maine are here, and invite a sojourn.

Old Orchard ranks with Cape May and Atlantic City in popularity with summer guests. It may be reached on the day of departure from Boston, in season for a six o'clock tea, by the ocean day-line in connection with trains at the Portland Union Station.

At the farther extremity of the city, reached also by street-cars, stands the station of the Grand Trunk Railway, whose trains offer another route to Poland Spring, to the Rangeley Region, and to the White Mountains.

Altogether Portland offers a variety of routes for reaching the many tourist points within the State, to which the water journey, the daylight sail from Boston, has been the breezy prelude.

Founded in 1632, under the Indian title Machigonne, the now city of Portland during the earlier days of settlement was the scene of many a fierce encounter between its hardy pioneers and the red men. After three bloody assaults the settlement finally, in the year 1689, succumbed to these Indian attacks, and those who escaped death by the tomahawk and arrow fled, leaving the deserted ruin of fort and home to bird and wild beast for a period of twenty-five years, when a number of sturdy veterans from the disbanded garrisons along the coast made their homes here, and when the Indians once more came down to pay their compliments they found a line of fortified streets and strong guards at every point.

The town now bore the name of Falmouth and enjoyed a flourishing commerce with the West Indies, when disaster again visited in the form of Captain Mowatt's British fleet, which sailed into its harbor one bright morning during the Revolutionary period — 1775 — and after a destructive bombardment of eight hours landed a party of red coats who fired all buildings spared by the red-hot shots of the ships. Falmouth again sank in ruins, yet to appear again, and as the reconstructed city of Portland go through a third fiery ordeal upon the "Glorious 4th," 1866, when a carelessly thrown fire-cracker started a conflagration, which, burning with fatal steadiness for sixteen hours, destroyed ten millions of property.

To-day, with a population approaching forty thousand, and a valuation of as many million of dollars, four daily newspapers, half a dozen national banks and thirty odd churches, surrounded by resting retreats of sea and shore, silvery-sanded beach and inland lake, this beautiful city, a carriage drive about which would amply repay a visit, whose large, well-kept hotels hold out a welcome to all, offers attractions to sojourn within its borders, or among its surroundings, which can but fill the time with pleasure.

CHAPTER FOURTH

EASTWARD AGAIN FROM PORTLAND — A CHARMING TWILIGHT RUN ALONG A HISTORIC COAST — THE MOUTH OF THE KENNEBEC, MONHEGAN ISLAND, ETC.

THE exit of the steamer from Portland harbor is, when the tide will allow, through the famous "White Head Passage," a narrow waterway formed by the approaching shores of Peak's and Cushing's islands. Upon the latter, and so near that, to use a nautical phrase, one could throw a biscuit to the steamer's deck, rises the towering height of White Head, one of the finest examples of the rugged coast of Maine existing. It recalls the lines —

> And many a homesick tear is shed
> By wanderers far away,
> As mem'ry reverts to "Old White Head,"
> And the islands of Casco Bay.

Upon the left Peak's Island, so close aboard that the music of its bands in pavilion and summer garden is borne to the steamer's deck, for this is the "Coney Island of the East," is the scene of merry revel. At unfavorable times of tide the passage out is through the ship channel, as we entered, and skirting the seaward shore of these islands.

These are the scenes which the inland traveller wots not of, and more follow in succession during the three hours of daylight which remains after leaving the Forest City.

Here are some of them: The passage through White Head leads directly to the sea, and the course is shaped just outside the fringe of islands, three hundred and sixty-five of which, by popular fable, are supposed to cluster within the encircling arms of Casco Bay, between the twin light upon Cape Elizabeth and the mouth of the Kennebec.

Unlike the islands in the harbor of Boston, arid, treeless and unadorned, Casco's Isles are forest crowned, with a primeval growth of pines and other northern woods, while, especially in the vicinity of Portland, they are adorned by the hand of man combined with Nature, and bear striking examples of summer architecture. Longfellow calls them —

> "The islands that were the Hesperides
> Of all my boyish dreams."

The cruise brings them into view, and with them the long peninsulas and deep indenting bays of Harpswell, as the steamer plows merrily along.

"Half-way Rock"—half-way between Portland and the Kennebec—is passed at this juncture; its tall light, a perfect Eddystone in its solitude, and its whistling buoy accompaniment in the foreground directly in the path of the steamer, which passes outside. Upon the mainland the shores of Old Falmouth rise to the elevation called Black-Strap Hill,—why Black-Strap tradition sayeth not,—which bears upon its summit a spindle erected by the United States Coast Survey as a land mark, to aid in their research. Travellers, strangers probably from the "Prairie States," have mistaken this for Mt. Washington. It is safe to assert that none who have made the journey by the ocean day-line from Boston, and witnessed the view from our strategic point, will be likely to confuse this mole-hill of Maine with the monarch of New Hampshire.

This will be a good point for reckoning—Item: Bring your field glasses and get the points of the compass fixed like a true sailor. Now, with the whistling buoy in direct line with Half-way Rock, pointing north, the whole panorama of Casco Bay is explained.

Just to the east of north the long peninsula of Harpswell projects far into the sea, island-surrounded upon all sides. To the west the larger islands of Chebeague, Long, The Diamonds, Peak's and Cushing's in succession, surround the harbor of Portland, shutting the city from view. The shores of Falmouth, Cumberland, Yarmouth and Freeport form the horizon.

After leaving Half-way Light, Martinicus Rock is the next objective point, in search of which the steamer soon rounds Cape Small Point, to find "Sequin" marking the approach to the mouth of the Kennebec, which noble river, famous world-wide for its ice product, flows from the clear depths of Moosehead Lake, in Northern Maine, until joining the waters of the Androscoggin, second only to itself, and forming the outlet of the Rangeley Lakes; the two from Merry-meeting Bay—suggestive name!—just above the coast line flow as one to find the sea at this point.

Its estuary forms the harbor of Boothbay, whose islands, Mouse and Squirrel, are summer-populated by hundreds of campers, cottagers and boarders. Boothbay Harbor forms the rendezvous of many a yachting party from metropolitan cities to and from eastern points.

We have met this white-winged craft, many of them in the voyage from Boston, for they are ever present in these summer waters, and include the entire ensemble of pleasure craft, from the tiny sloop to stately schooners, cup-winners, with the floating palaces of the Bennetts, Goulds and Astors; for all favor this picturesque coast, each season cruising Eastward, Ho!

Leaving Sequin, with its stately light, one of the many beacons of which Whittier says:

> "From gray sea fog, from icy drift,
> From peril and from pain;
> The home-bound fisher greets thy lights
> O hundred-harbored Maine!"

Monhegan next comes to the front. O for space to pick up some of the many threads of history connected with the steamer's surroundings as she plows along this coast, events dating back prior to the landing of the Pilgrims, for it was Samoset, a chieftain of Monhegan, who, at Plymouth, met the Puritans with the English words, "Welcome! Whitemen!"

Monhegan is the most famous island on the New England coast; it appears upon the oldest charts in existence, and to it the earliest voyagers to the Western Continent converged. Champlain sailed the Des Monts expedition to this point in 1604. Weymouth was here in 1607, trading with the Indians of Pemaquid. Pemaquid, the ancient fortified city, which to this day forms the goal of historian and antiquarian, the Pompeii of the West. These delve in her paved streets and unearth her old fortifications, enthusiastically recalling scenes which have added pages to our early history.

Between Monhegan and the mainland of Pemaquid Point was fought that desperately contested sea-fight between the Enterprise and Boxer, familiar to every school-boy of the land. The English brig Boxer had been fitted out with the express purpose of engaging the Enterprise, an American brig of her own class and armament. The Enterprise had seen service in the wars with Algiers, and now called home by the War of 1812, was given a cruising ground along the coast of Maine to keep watch for the enemy's privateers.

Decatur had been her commander, but she was now taken to sea by Lieutenant Burrows, an intrepid seaman, of whom it was believed he would die sooner than surrender. After terrorizing the seacoast villages, and firing a fisherman or two, the Boxer cast anchor Saturday, September 4, 1814, in Pemaquid Bay.

On the morning of the Sabbath, calm, clear and beautiful as a September morning in these seas can be, the lookout from the Boxer descried the Enterprise bearing down from Portland under full sail. In a moment all was activity on board the Englishman, who, dropping a few shots upon the village and old Fort Frederick by way of compliment, up anchor and away to a point about three miles from shore and then stripped to fighting canvas. The Enterprise coming up noted the invitation, and cleared for action.

In expectancy of this event both ships had been prepared by their crews, rubbed down and polished off with as much care as a pugilist receives from his trainers ; so earnest were those of the Boxer, that her colors were nailed to the mast, an act which doubtless cost some lives in the event which followed.

The fight lasted forty minutes ; and so closely were the ships engaged that after the first broadsides nothing could be seen of the combatants, save the flash of the guns through the thick veil of smoke which enveloped all. When the fire slackened the Enterprise was seen to be the victor. Both commanders were killed outright ; and on the 7th the Enterprise, with the Boxer in tow, set sail for Portland, where equal honors were bestowed upon the dead. Wrapped each in his country's colors, the dead captains were borne to their final resting place in the ancient cemetery, under the shadow of the observatory which we saw crowning the eastern extremity of the city of Portland as we entered its harbor.

The roar of combat was plainly heard through the Sabbath stillness of the Forest City, and Longfellow refers to it thus in his poem, "My Lost Youth" ;

> "I remember the sea-fight far away,
> How it thundered o'er the tide !
> And the dead captains, as they lay
> In their graves, o'erlooking the tranquil bay,
> Where they together died."

Through scenes, the theatre of such events, the steamer makes its way, during the long twilight of summer, and now as the coast lights beam through the gathering gloom one by one her voyagers "seek the seclusion that the *stateroom* grants," where, surrounded by the invigorating air, blown from the wide salt sea, amid odors such as no landsman knows, they sink to rest, wooed by a quiet broken, yet not disturbed, by the dull, far away throb of the engines and the wash of the waves. There are no noisy landings, with their accompanying discharge of freight, to disturb refreshing slumber, which may continue until the landing at Eastport at 7.30 next morning.

CHAPTER FIFTH

PASSAMAQUODDY AND ABOUT THERE — EASTPORT AND ITS SURROUNDINGS — HOW TO REACH GRAND MANAN, CAMPOBELLO, LUBEC, ETC. — A SUMMER CAMP.

UNRUFFLED Passamaquoddy Bay lies sheltered from the sea by a mighty chain of islands, all British territory, for this is the eastern extremity of the United States.

Its shores and islands bear numerous summer resorts, which possess enough of individuality to warrant a separate and detailed description. At favorable times of tide, when it "serves," to use a nautical phrase, the route of the International steamers into Passamaquoddy is through "The Narrows," formed by Lubec, a white, wooded town upon the left and the long island of Campobello to the right. The entrance to this channel is past the light at "Quoddy Head," which marks the eastern limit of the United States of America.

At other seasons of the tide one must circumnavigate Campobello, and approach the American town of Eastport through British waters. The magnificent sweep of Passamaquoddy Bay must be seen to be thoroughly appreciated. Its encircling shores form a horizon seventy-

five miles in circumference, all of which from some one of its many elevations, as the Chamcook Mountains above St. Andrews, is brought into one view. It forms an arm of the Bay of Fundy, and partakes of its high tides, while its breezy summited islands exclude its fogs.

These phenomenal tides rise and fall twice daily in Passamaquoddy, measuring between thirty and forty feet, while to the eastward they go still higher. The rivers which find the sea within the Bay of Fundy are said to part of the time run up hill, part down, as the tide swells them.

There are few islands in the Bay of Passamaquoddy after passing through the outer fringe which shelters its quiet waters. One of these, Minister's Island, which lies off the peninsula of St. Andrews, fitly exemplifies these tides. Between this island and the mainland there exists at the flood an exact half mile of clear water. At the ebb tide one can ride or walk, dry shod, over a bar of shingle connecting the two, *twenty feet below the level of the sea at high water.*

Passamaquoddy is the ideal spot for summer sojourn. Beside the historical interest, blending romance with the beautiful in nature, it has a peculiar charm for health-seekers in its pleasant air. There is no fog, the encircling islands shut out that unwelcome visitor from the sea; the powerful tides remove all refuse far from shore twice each day, and last, but not least, there is the assurance given by General A. W. Greeley, chief of the United States Signal Service, which has such a bearing on the subject of climatic perfection in this locality that we quote it.

In an article in "Scribner's," entitled "Where shall we spend our summers?" after detailing what people are led to expect from reading summer literature descriptive of this and that resort, General Greeley says: "There is possibly one place in the United States where such conditions obtain, — a bit of country of about forty square miles at the extreme southwestern part of the United States, in which San Diego is situated; but even here, perhaps once in two or three years, the sultry blasts from the Mojave Desert pass over the low mountain range and parch this favored district. . . . . By a singular contrast the second favored spot as to summer weather is the extreme northeastern point of the United States, — Eastport, Maine. . . . . At Eastport, the prevailing summer winds are from the south, which makes the weather delightful." General Greeley, in the charts which accompany his article, places the mean daily temperature at 68° during the entire heated term. There is another phase of summer weather which is of equal importance with the question of temperature. This is a humidity of atmosphere. Again we quote Gen. Greeley, whose chart shows that the belt denoting the dryest atmosphere passes through Passamaquoddy Bay. He says: "It is further of importance to note that the quantity of vapor per cubic foot decreases as one goes northward, and the absolute amount of water in the air in New Jersey is fifty per cent greater than in Maine, while the quantity along the Atlantic seacoast from Hatteras south is nearly twice as great. . . . A dry summer climate is assumed to be one where the atmosphere contains five and one-half grains or less of aqueous vapor to each cubic foot (our belt has only five grains), and on this basis it is safe to recommend the northern half of New England and New York." Gen. Greeley can be considered an impartial writer, having no climatic wares to dispose of. In naming Eastport, he named the extreme limit of his country and consequently of his research ; therefore as Eastport, so Passamaquoddy and about there.

A PASSAMAQUODDY INCIDENT.

Immediately following the California gold fever of 1849, a far-reaching, notable enterprise was inaugurated in Passamaquoddy.

In 1850-51 the steamer S. B. Wheeler, a side-wheeled wooden craft, in size and tonnage resembling the "Rose Standish" of the Frontier Steamboat Line, whose steamers now ply the waters of the bay and river St. Croix, was built at Eastport. Up the river St. Croix, at the towns of Calais, Maine, and St. Stephen, New Brunswick, which we shall see later, on opposite banks of the river, was built upon the English side the barque Fanny, with an object in view of curious nature.

The hull of this vessel was towed to Eastport, the captain of the "Cumberland," one of the International fleet, — perchance our very ship — forming one of the crew of the tow.

Here she was sunk, after removing the entire stern of the craft, for in her construction this part had been secured by screw bolts for this express purpose, and while submerged the steamer was floated within and secured by ballast and freight tightly packing the entire hold of the barque. Then the Fanny was raised, her stern once more secured, her hold freed from water, her masts stepped, two of them passing directly through the steamer, her rigging and sails supplied, and out of Passamaquoddy she sailed "'round The Horn" to San Francisco.

Arrived there, the same process was carried out for the removal of the steamer, which, reconstructed, sailed for years the Sacramento river, the first river steamer in California waters.

No part of the steamer was removed when she was engulfed within the barque, save her funnel and walking-beam. She furnished accommodations for the passengers taken out in this way, and possibly some forty-niners of the Pacific coast may yet remain of those who made the voyage in this novel manner.

EASTPORT, MAINE.

Eastport, prominent upon the school maps as the extreme eastern settlement under the American flag, prominent in history of old-time boundary disputes, and the home of the American sardine, is situated upon Moose Island, at the entrance of Passamaquoddy Bay, separated by a wooden bridge twelve hundred feet in length from the mainland town of Perry.

It is a town of white wooden buildings, a big hotel flying the American flag, an exceedingly peaceful-looking arsenal, a fort and a United States Coaling Station.

Along its water front the many wharves are occupied by numerous factories, where minute herring are cooked in salad oil, packed in cans exactly resembling the conventional sardine box, and placed on the market, a close imitation of the imported article, whose market price they have greatly cheapened. Fourteen of these sardine factories lie within the radius of a circle drawn one-half mile from the post-office. They simply line the water front. Previous to the fire of 1886 there were twenty-one factories in Eastport, with an average capacity of twenty hogsheads of uncooked fish per day, representing some 800,000 boxes. Of course, fish in quantities to allow this were not to be had every day, but during the season, May 15th to December 1st, enormous quantities of the fish are caught in the weirs which surround the inlets to the bay, and cured. Fish that, going in as herring, undergo a metamorphosis, coming out sardines. This is a specialty of the eastern shore, in which Eastport bears the palm.

As is customary in smaller towns, every modern event in Eastport dates from "the fire," a conflagration that, in 1886, swept the larger part of the town into ruins. The effect of the destruction has, on the whole, been beneficial to its appearance, as the new buildings are greatly superior to the old, and an efficient system of water-works has since been introduced, while a Government building, — custom house, — for which Congress has appropriated $100,000, is in course of erection. This town forms the principal trade centre of the frontier. "The Quoddy" is its leading hotel.

Here the International Steamship Company has made special provisions for traffic and travel, in its large depot built since the fire. At this point its steamers land, and by connecting water routes by other boats of lighter draught, the traveller is carried to the resorts in Passamaquoddy and its environs, to Campobello and famous Grand Manan, to St. Andrews, and the towns of the St. Croix River. The Passamaquoddy tribe of Indians from their home, a reservation upon Pleasant Point just above Eastport, add a picturesque element to the life of the town. Their bark canoes still ply the waters of the bay in their periodical visits to the several summer resorts. They may, with profit to themselves and the sportsman, serve as guides in canoeing, hunting, and fishing excursions in the vicinity, from their aboriginal knowledge of woodcraft and the famous lurking places of fish and game.

NORTH LUBEC.

Adjoining Eastport, reached by steam ferry across the harbor, lies the town of Lubec, approaching Campobello, and reaching northward in a series of long peninsulas, characteristic of this rugged eastern shore.

It is upon one of these sea-girt necks of land, all surrounded by Cobscook Bay, and near neighbor to the famous resorts of Passamaquoddy, that the site for the permanent summer encampment of the Young Men's Christian Association has been chosen.

Two years ago, a committee was selected by the New England Association to search out and report upon an advantageous site. North Lubec was chosen, and unanimously endorsed by the annual convention.

The initial encampment was held August 10th to 25th, 1889. It was a complete success. Without exception all were pleased with the selection, and the continuance of the encampment at North Lubec was assured.

Leading Association men have since purchased a large tract of land for the purpose of developing the encampment. A large hotel has been erected, in which ample accommodations for visitors are provided. Bowling alleys, tennis courts and base-ball field afford opportunities for amusement and exercise.

Thus, amid the health-giving breezes from the sea, this association has a rallying-place, after the plan of the Maine Chautauquans upon another border, that between Maine and New Hampshire, at Fryeburg.

CUTLER, MAINE.

It is only of late that Cutler Harbor has come to the front as a summer resort, from its secluded position on the coast of Maine. It lies midway between Mt. Desert and Passamaquoddy in a sheltered bay, which has proved so attractive that a syndicate of gentlemen have purchased the lands about its shores, built a modern summer hotel upon improved sanitary conditions, and laid out their lands into sites for numerous mansions, cottages and tastefully planned parks.

Go where you will, by land or water, by carriage or sail, or rambling along the shore or in the woods, objects of interest continually meet the eye. Prominent among these are the Natural Bridge, Cross Island, the Norse Wall and Lake, the foot-prints on the rocks, caves, lakes, streams and water-falls, the lighthouse and life-saving station, the mineral springs and meadow views. It offers all the attractions of the secluded coast resort, "far from the madding crowd," its little gem of a harbor receiving many white-winged yachts during the season which bring hither many summer guests.

PEMBROKE, PERRY, DENNYSVILLE AND ROBBINSTON.

Upon the western shore of Passamaquoddy, above Lubec, lies the town of Perry, containing Pleasant Point, a village of the Passamaquoddy tribe of Indians. Pembroke adjoins Perry upon the west, and Robbinston lies just above upon the St. Croix.

These are all coast towns bordering the bay and river, with a multiplicity of projecting peninsulas and encroaching bays, affording fine salt-water fishing, while their forests abound with game.

CAMPOBELLO.

This Elysium of the summer tourist is his first resort "over the border," in reaching which, from Eastport, one and one-half miles by steam ferry, he crosses that imaginary line, the International boundary. The island is picturesque with coves and cliffs, winding roads and woods, a series of delightful surprises to the uninitiated. One may remain out of doors the entire day without sense of fatigue or heat, so clear, bracing and cool is the sea atmosphere. Fog never remains the entire day, and during the last five seasons there has been not more than three days each summer month in which it was impossible to walk or drive, while the beauty of the landscape is wonderfully increased by the shutting down and lifting of the mists.

> "A wind came up out of the sea,
> And said, O mists, make room for me!"

Campobello and Deer islands are the larger of the islands which shut out the sea from Passamaquoddy. Campobello has been chosen before its mates as an island summer resort from its beauty and grandeur of situation.

Upon its shores begins the wild scenery of the Bay of Fundy, a name sonorous as its waves, which wash the beetling cliffs upon the outer shore of Campobello. The fine model hotel, Ty'n-y-coed, is happily situated upon one of these cliffs, seventy-five feet above the level of the sea, and near the water's edge. It is provided with all the comforts of a refined

home, and is beautifully furnished throughout. Its seaward view embraces a wide sweep of ocean, broken only by the purple cliffs of Grand Manan; shoreward the hilly towns of Eastport and Lubec are in the view, which also holds the Denny's River and the famous St. Croix with varied vistas of Passamaquoddy reaches through forest-crowned islands that intercept it.

Campobello partakes with Eastport in the history of old-time boundary disputes, and British occupancy of all the islands in the bay during the four years, 1814-18, that all remained under martial law. The English claimed that all belonged to Great Britain, as much so, to quote one of their commissioners, as Northamptonshire, an inland county of England.

It had been a muddle since the treaty of 1783, at the close of the Revolutionary war — a muddle which required thirty-five years of diplomatic squabbling to clear. Finally, under an article of the treaty of Ghent, concluded December 24, 1814, two commissioners were appointed to settle the vexed question of ownership; their final report states "that Moose Island, Dudley Island, and Frederick Island, in the Bay of Passamaquoddy, do belong to the United States, and that all the other islands in the bay and the island of Grand Manan, in the Bay of Fundy, belong to His Britannic Majesty." Thus the Union Jack floats over Campobello with its merry summer company, and that storm-defying ocean monarch, Grand Manan.

GRAND MANAN.

This noble island, "a paradise of sea-girt cliffs," as some writer has termed it, lies in the very entrance to the Bay of Fundy, nine miles from the American shore and eighteen miles from Eastport, where steamers may be taken for reaching it, by easy sail of two hours.

For a long time Grand Manan has been a favorite resort for marine artists and others interested in grand cliff and shore scenery.

The highest and most precipitous cliffs are at the southern extremity of the island. Here they rise to a height of from three to four hundred feet above the sea, which breaks at their feet with sullen roar and spray dashed high against the mighty barrier, dislodging myriads of sea-fowl, which wing their screaming flight below. It is a scene which reminds one of the tales of the Norwegian coast, or what might be expected in Icelandic waters or among the Hebrides.

The western shore extends in a series of these cliffs twenty miles, with no accessible entrance from the sea; but on the eastern shore are several villages lying within pleasant coves; smaller islands lie scattered in the sea off shore upon this side.

Near the northern head, called Bishop's Head, from a rocky figure rising boldly out of the sea off shore, and named "The Bishop," are two hotels and some private boarding-houses. In this neighborhood is Swallow-tail Head, upon which the lighthouse stands, surrounded by cliffs deeply scarred by the action of the waves.

Whale Cove opens delightful features; around it tower gigantic cliffs displaying a variety of formations, at one place brilliant with varied hues, and in another regular strata are piled up in consecutive layers, commonly called the "Seven Days' Work." The beaches at the foot of the cliffs show gay-colored pebbles.

It is a land of wonderment, and presents, especially during and following a storm, marine views unsurpassed in their grandeur. There are good facilities for fishing and shooting. The roads of the island are excellent; good horses for driving can be had at moderate prices, and the same may be said of boats and boatmen.

It is a land which should be visited by all lovers of the sublime in Nature, and may be taken in as a side trip with the other Passamaquoddy resorts in the ocean voyage eastward.

WHALE COVE
— GRAND MANAN —

ST. ANDREWS.

> "And the pale health-seeker findeth there
> The wine of life in its pleasant air."

This couplet might well have been written of the charming new-old summer-resort, St. Andrews-by-the-sea; old, dating back far beyond its early settlement by the sturdy Loyalists, who fled from America upon the Declaration of Independence, issued by the colonies, and who founded upon the long peninsula extending far into the bay, this quaint old town, whose streets laid out by Deputy John Jones, surveyor for the Crown, in 1784, are the earliest example of the Philadelphia checkerboard plan on record, consisting of avenues of a uniform length and fifty to eighty feet wide, crossing at right angles and dividing the town into sixty blocks, each three hundred and twenty feet square.

Old again in its reminiscences of its sturdy Loyalist fore-fathers, who, leaving the "States" during and immediately following their rebellion against the Crown, brought to this quiet border town their families and flocks, with, in some cases, their homes also, in proof of which there are houses now standing in St. Andrews whose frames were brought from Castine by their Loyalist owners, and set up anew beneath the Crown.

Within the English church of the town rests, conspicuously displayed, the royal coat-of-arms, brought by its staunch supporter, Parson Samuel Andrews, from the church at Wallingford, Connecticut, where, during the struggle for independence, he had earnestly prayed for the success of the English arms, and, caring not to live in the new republic, settled at St. Andrews, bringing the emblem of royalty with him.

New St. Andrews boasts its fine hotel, "The Algonquin," opened in June, 1889, to receive nearly 1,400 guests its first season, and other improvements of the old town, which have made this sleeping-beauty of the seaside the ideal summer resort.

Few coast towns have a more favored location than St. Andrews. Long before it was thought of as a summer resort, it enjoyed a certain patronage from pleasure-seekers from Northern New Brunswick and across the border. Its marked characteristics led to the formation of the St. Andrews Land Company, who have, with their varied improvements, of which the new hotel and Indian Point Park are notable examples, made the old town to blossom like the rose.

The hotel stands upon an eminence overlooking the town, and 150 feet above sea level. From its broad piazzas an unobstructed view is had, disclosing the whole panorama of Passamaquoddy Bay, with the Chamcook Mountains, the St. Croix River and the distant shores of Nova Scotia for a background.

Its guests enjoy a wonderful immunity from hay fever, that distressing malady being unknown to the residents of the town, while the afflicted, even those who visit here at well-advanced stages of the disorder, find early and complete relief.

It is pleasant to write of St. Andrews. To one who has visited it there is always much to recall with pleasure; while with the ocean voyage from Boston, or from Portland to Eastport, as an auxiliary, no better medicine can be recommended the tired brain-worker, or summer health and pleasure-seeker, than a sojourn at this Passamaquoddy resort. There are mountains for climbing, the Chameooks, reached in a three-mile drive from the hotel, over roads which are perfection, and at their feet lie a chain of clear water lakes affording fine trout fishing. Angling in both salt and fresh water may be enjoyed here with sure result. The yatchsman finds a paradise, and the student of history his desire. There are possibilities for pleasure to suit every taste, coupled with a quiet restfulness of surroundings which is itself a boon.

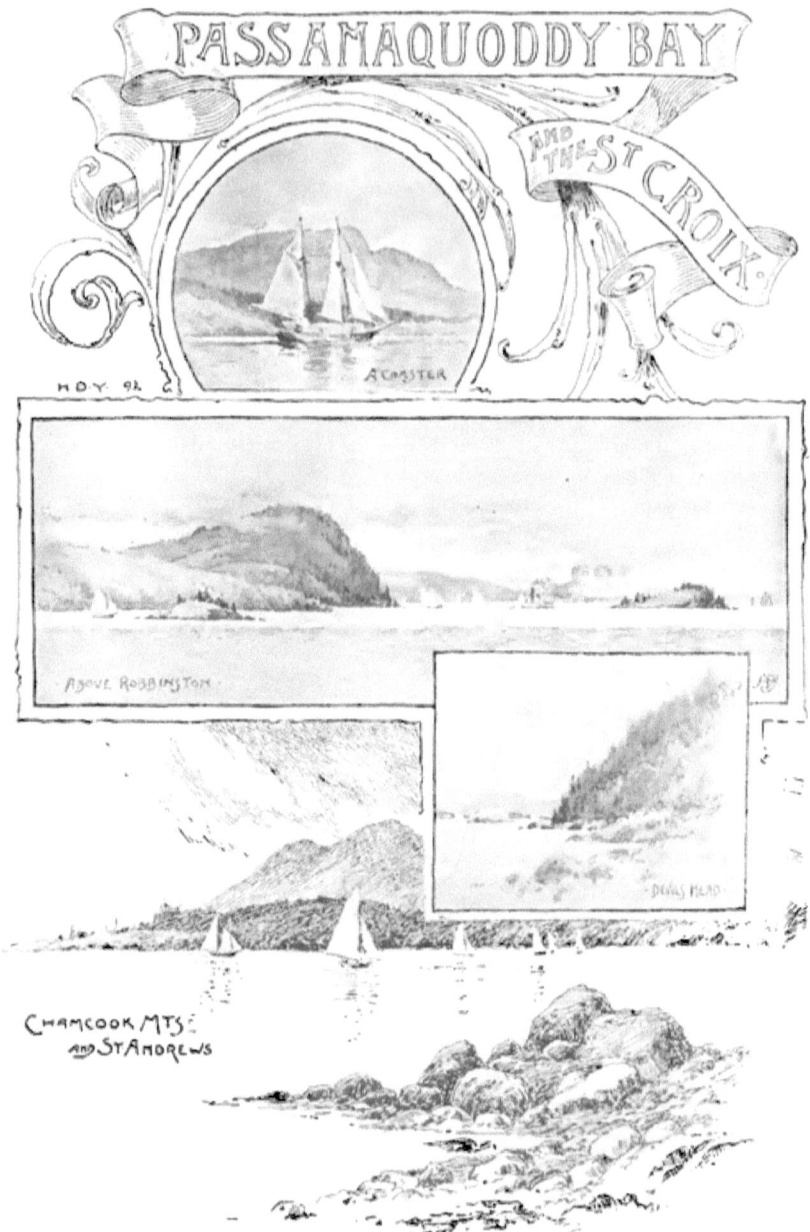

CHAPTER SIXTH

THE ST. CROIX RIVER AND SCHOODIC LAKES, THE SPORTSMAN'S PARADISE — A STORY OF 1604 — CALAIS AND ST. STEPHEN, THE GATE TO THE PROVINCES.

IT IS the Frontier Steamboat Company, whose boats, connecting with the International steamers at the wharf of the latter company at Eastport, cross the bay to St. Andrews and ascend the historic St. Croix to the river towns along its banks. It is thirteen miles to St. Andrews — thirteen miles of delightful sailing with the objective point in view, backed up by the Chamcook Mountains and other highlands of New Brunswick, which border the bay.

After leaving the wharf at St. Andrews, the steamer rounds Joe's Point and enters the St. Croix. This noble stream flows from the Chiputneticook, or Schoodic chain of lakes — lakes famous for their fishing and hunting opportunities — and forms, with the lakes above named, for a considerable distance the boundary line between the United States and Dominion of Canada. This is *the* region for famous game and fish — the home of the moose, deer and land-locked salmon.

Ascending the St. Croix as far as Calais, a point we shall soon reach in description, which lies thirty miles up river from Eastport, a short railroad, the St. Croix & Penobscot, may be taken, which will bear the sportsman twice across the river and on to the village of Princeton at the very outlet of the Grand Lakes of Washington County, Maine, and into a game region of forest, lake and stream.

From Princeton a small steamboat runs up the lower lake to Grand Lake Stream, the outlet of Grand Lake, and the home of countless land-locked salmon of aldermanic proportions. On the lower lake there is a large village of Passamaquoddy Indians, whose young men make capital guides for the sportsmen entering this region.

The townships here bear numbers as distinctive marks: settlements have not driven out the game, which here exists as in no other part of the State. The Maine Commissioner of Game and Fish has recently placed the number of deer "on the hoof" within his territory at ten thousand, with a large ratio at home within these Washington County woods. The names of Grand Lake and Grand Lake Stream are a well-known and sufficient guarantee that the angler may here find *Ultima Thule.*

Can a more delightful trip be planned by the sportsman than the ocean voyage we have described, reaching Eastport in the early morning after twenty-four restful hours from Boston, and with the privilege of sojourn in Passamaquoddy if desired, or push on to this sportsman's paradise by boat and rail same day?

But to return to the ascent of the St. Croix, from which we have been diverted by these sporting possibilities. Joe's Point hides the town of St. Andrews, and the little steamer bears away up stream with Europe on the right and the border of America to the left. America presents the shores of Robbinston and reminds of the current border story of a cannon-ball dropped into St. Andrews' suburbs upon the 4th of July, and returned upon the Queen's Birthday. As the distance from town to town is three miles, this must resolve itself into popular fable, told for its border-poetic effect. In truth, there is only harmony between the two.

Chamcook Mountains, upon the New Brunswick side, are soon passed, and Douchet's Island appears in mid channel. Here description must give way to historical incident, which must wake the dullest fancy as one passes this small island, so long neutral territory, and which is fast disappearing before the flow of the stream, which must ere long remove this, the site of the earliest attempt at settlement in this part of the New World. Here is the story : —

By royal patent given by King Henry IV. — Henry of Navarre — and dated November 8, 1603, all the American territory between the fortieth and forty-sixth degree of north latitude was granted to his well-beloved friend Pierre de Gast, the Sieur Des Monts. "Acadia" was the name given to the grant — a name which still clings to the country and people : thus we have the Acadians, and the towns of Tracadie, Shubenacadie and others in Nova Scotia.

Des Monts during the winter secured and equipped two vessels, in which he and his party arrived the 6th of May, 1604, on the southerly side of the peninsula of Nova Scotia. Coasting the new country they entered the beautiful Annapolis basin, where, charmed with the spot, part of the expedition remained to found the ancient town of Port Royal. — now Annapolis, Nova Scotia. We shall see this town later on, and present a picture of the defences erected by this early colony.

Des Monts, with Samuel Champlain as pilot, set sail for fresh discoveries in the new acquisition. They explored the Bay of Fundy, and thence proceeded to the waters of Passamaquoddy, which they called a "sea of salt water." This was the first expedition to these waters. Passing through the outer fringe of islands, which stand guard as to-day, sheltering the calm within from the boisterous sea without, the ships crossed the bay, passing within pistol shot of the site of the present town of St. Andrews, and ascended the St. Croix, even as we now are, until arriving at a small island Champlain selected it as a suitable spot for defence, disembarked his forces and fortified it against encroachment from the Indians.

He, geographer as well as pilot, describes it as "about three leagues in circuit," and from the fact that immediately above small streams flowed crosswise to join the larger river, thus giving it the form of the Holy Cross, he named the island St. Croix, a name which has since descended to the river, while Douchet's is the name the island bears.

During the long boundary disputes this island was held as neutral ground and enjoyed all the rights and privileges of *No Man's Land*, thus becoming a favored dueling resort.

To-day it bears a light supported by the United States Government. Within the keeper's house are many relics of the early settlement.

Upon this island Des Monts chose to winter the expedition. The Indians were disposed to be friendly to the strangers, but of this the colonists were in doubt and took every precaution to guard against surprise. Prodigality in building their winter quarters had caused a dearth of wood, and as the long, cold winter of the northern climate progressed, the water-courses were frozen and the men were forced to cross to the mainland for both wood and water. This they did under cover of the night and in constant fear of attack.

To add to the horror of their situation a new and dread disease broke out among them. Thirty-six of the little band of ninety fell victims to scurvy before a remedy was found in a simple antiscorbutic — the boughs of the spruce steeped and drank. This was recommended by the Indians, and forms the earliest testimonial in favor of *spruce beer*.

The bodies of their dead were carried at night to the mainland by their comrades and there buried. Fancy the feelings of these men in a new and unexplored country, in the midst of an unknown death, and surrounded by a dreaded forest foe!

Spring came at last to their relief, and, with the survivors, Des Monts set sail about the middle of May, 1605, southward in search of a warmer clime. They entered the Penobscot, discovered and named Mount Desert, and voyaged as far as Cape Cod; there the search was abandoned and the ship returned to Port Royal.

THE MAGAGUADAVIC RIVER AND LAKE UTOPIA.

Let us return for a moment to Passamaquoddy before bidding it adieu.
At a point some distance east of the peninsula occupied by St. Andrews, the Magaguadavic River, a purely provincial stream, finds the sea also in Passamaquoddy Bay. It bears a strong part in the history of boundary disputes. For more than a century and a half following the attempted colonization at the island of the Holy Cross, this was practically a forgotten region. Meanwhile, other adventurers from Catholic France had visited the Magaguadavic, and, as was the custom with discoverers from Catholic countries, had set up the cross at its mouth. From this incident the river became known as the St. Croix, and as such when confounded with the St. Croix of the Des Monts expedition, which was named as the boundary in the treaty of peace between Great Britain and the United States, at the close of the revolutionary struggle, caused the knot which required so much diplomacy to unravel.

The river flows from a lake of the same name, near Magaguadavic station on the New Brunswick Railway, and receives numerous affluents on its way to the sea. Its course is through rural New Brunswick, a country of fields and forests.

Lake Utopia lies near the coast, where in early days the Indians had their homes and rallying-place. Curious relics of this aboriginal people are from time to time unearthed. The overflow of its waters reach the Magaguadavic River through a natural canal and enter the bay at St. George, with a rush of waters known as the Falls of the Magaguadavic, a picturesque cascade well worth a visit.

On the west shore of the lake rises a palisade of rock, a peculiarly beautiful red granite much sought in architectural adornment.

Here the St. George Granite Company quarries from the everlasting hills fine building stone, and here we take leave of Passamaquoddy.

CALAIS AND ST. STEPHEN.

Leaving Douchet's Island behind, the steamer ascends the St. Croix to the head of navigation, thirty miles above Eastport, where are the two important points, the city of Calais, Maine, upon the left and the town of St. Stephen, New Brunswick, upon the right bank.

The American city of Calais is the largest and most important point in Eastern Maine, and St. Stephen the leading town on the Canadian side of the river.

The prominent industry of both is the manufacture of lumber, for which the magnificent water power of the St. Croix affords unrivalled facilities, and the upper section on each side is known as Milltown. These places are connected by bridges, and, though under different national and local governments, have common interests, and together constitute a large community, the most important centre of commercial and industrial pursuits between the Penobscot and the St. John. Besides the flourishing lumber trade, each has also considerable shipping interests. At Milltown, on the Canadian side, stands a large cotton factory, erected principally by American capital and controlled by American management; and at Red Beach, in the lower ward of Calais, are quarries which produce red granite, a beautiful building material, also widely used for monumental purposes.

The sites of the two places, sloping upward on opposite shores, afford fine locations for the homes, business places, and public buildings of the prosperous people. Among them are the steeples of elegant church edifices, and excellent hotels accommodate the large travel which centres in the wide-awake community.

There are interesting drives about the two towns, in the enjoyment of which the American visitor must be taught the unwritten law of provincial roads, which requires the driver to turn to the *left* in passing, the direct opposite to the rule of the road in the "States," but the correct thing, as it brings the drivers side by side, thus narrowing the possibility of collision.

> "The rule of the road is a paradox quite,
> In driving your carriage along,
> If you keep to the left, you are sure to go right,
> If you keep to the right you go wrong."

As this rule of the road is prevalent throughout the British Provinces, we give it here at the doorway.

Both St. Stephens, at this point on the river, and St. Andrews at its mouth, present routes for reaching Northern Maine and New Brunswick points, being branch terminals of the New Brunswick Railway. These branches join at Watt Junction, some twenty miles above the St. Croix, and afford the shortest route to the New Brunswick towns of McAdam, Magaguadavic, Canterbury, Benton, Debec and Woodstock, and the Maine town of Houlton. A continuation of the branch from Debec Junction strikes the main line of the road at Newburgh, near Woodstock, reaching the Aroostook County (Maine) towns of Fort Fairfield, Caribou and Presque Isle, as well as all Northern New Brunswick towns to the Madawaska River.

But St. John forms the true gateway through which to reach all Provincial points, and to St. John the International steamers, from Eastport, next proceed to meet connections by rail over the New Brunswick and Intercolonial railways with all parts of the Old North-East.

FISHING BOATS

MOUNT DESERT HILLS, AS SEEN FROM INTERNATIONAL STEAMERS.

CHAPTER SEVENTH

UP THE BAY OF FUNDY TO THE CHIEF CITY OF NEW BRUNSWICK — FALLS OF THE ST. JOHN RIVER — SPORT IN ABUNDANCE — PRETTY FREDERICTON, ETC.

IT IS a daylight sail through the British waters of the Bay of Fundy to St. John, the steamer keeping close to shore, allowing the New Brunswick coast to pass in moving panorama. Here and there a rocky cove appears, giving way to pretty bay and pebbly beach, inhabited as rude isolated cabin and tidy settlement indicates. As the steamer advances into the bay the interest deepens.

Warner says: "The very name of Fundy is stimulating to the imagination amid the geographical wastes of youth. The young fancy reaches out to its tides with an enthusiasm that is given only to Fingal's Cave and other pictorial wonders of the text-book. I am sure the district schools would become what they are not now if the geographers would make other parts of the globe as attractive as the sonorous Bay of Fundy."

ST. JOHN.

After steaming eastward for three and one-half hours we enter the harbor of St. John, and approach the city. This harbor is deep and capacious. It lies upon the western and southern sides of the city, with Partridge Island, upon which are a light, signal and quarantine station, sheltering it from the sea. St. John is the maritime city of the Maritime Provinces. Its wharves and docks are ever thronged with shipping, for vast quantities of lumber, the product of New Brunswick forests, are annually sent from this trade centre of the lower provinces, which has become the fourth among the shipping ports of the world.

The city is made up of the municipal district of St. John proper, the city of Portland and the suburb of Fairville, with but imaginary lines of division. Altogether they contain a population of fifty thousand. At its wharves the famous tides rise and fall thirty feet, seeming to produce a tempering effect on the summer atmosphere; an oppressively warm day is of rare occurrence, the evenings and nights being delightfully cool, and the air filled with "the odor of brine from the ocean."

St. John is well provided with hotels, the Royal, the Dufferin and Victoria being examples, and being the chief city of New Brunswick, to it converge all rail and steam navigation lines of this "*East Countree.*"

Visitors to the city much enjoy the fine drives amid its surroundings. One of these leads across the suspension bridge, and affords a fine view of the "reversible cataract" which exists where river meets sea.

Think of the immense volume of water which the St. John River discharges into the sea, all emptied through a narrow rocky chasm but 500 feet wide. Just above the city the river expands into a broad bay with every intention of a quiet exit from its confining banks. But just above the city, where, at their narrowest point, two bridges have been built, one a foot and carriage suspension and the other a railroad canti-

IN ST JOHN HARBOR.

lever, the waters are confined in a rugged gorge, through which they rush with the speed and power of a mill-race. Here occurs the fall. It is a peculiar fall, and the above term applied to it by an American humorist explains its peculiarity. At high tide the sea has a descent of fifteen feet into the river; at low tide the river has a like fall into the sea; at half-tide all is serene, and the river may be navigated with safety. This is above St. John, and does not affect the seaward approach to the city.

Of historical interest St. John possesses much. Near the bridges, upon the Carleton side of the harbor, one may see the ruins of Fort La Tour, where was enacted the grandest drama of woman's heroism ever enacted in the New World. Madame La Tour and her famous defence of the fort and garrison which occupied this spot will be remembered as long as Canada has a history.

Then one must visit the Martello Tower — old stone towers are not so common that this can be overlooked — one of the ancient defences of the city, crowning the hill upon the harbor front, and climb the steep hill of Fort Howe, at the western extremity of the city, to obtain the bird's-eye view of St. John, its environs and lively harbor scene, which is presented at its best from this point.

Fort Howe now contains a few antiquated cannon and dismantled barracks, but time was when it presented all the lively phases of an English garrison, and there remain many evidences of its military occupation. Notable troops were quartered here. The sunburned heroes of the Crimea; soldiers, who had fought at Inkerman and in the trenches before Sebastopol, were quartered amid these quiet surroundings in ye olden time.

St. John's public and private buildings are, as a rule, of fine appearance, and the new passenger railway station used by the Intercolonial and New Brunswick roads is a model of modern taste and convenience.

Altogether, St. John's invitation may well be heeded, and a brief sojourn, at least, before farther journeying may be passed with pleasure and profit within her borders.

This, then, forms the terminus of the International Line, three hundred and fifty miles from Boston, and as the steamers, finding a ready passenger list of provincial people and returning tourists, retrace the route to Boston, we are left at St. John to consider in which direction our pilgrimage shall now lead us.

THE RIVER ST. JOHN.

First let us consider the St. John River, its villages, towns, cities, and hunting and fishing resorts, reached by the New Brunswick Railway from St. John City.

Rising in Northern Maine this noble stream, justly celebrated for its scenery, flows northward then toward the east forming for many miles the International boundary, until finally, with one grand sweep around the northern highlands, it begins its course of three hundred miles to the sea. It and its tributaries drain an immense area in Maine, New Brunswick and Quebec, reaching out to forest lakes though a timber growth which is yet a stranger to the woodsman's axe. Within these shaded wilds are large game and large fish, to test the nerve and skill of the sportsman.

Along the main stream farm succeeds farm for miles, on either bank, interspersed by town and village of rural quiet. Its head waters penetrate the Province of Quebec, and approach the famous salmon streams Restigouche and Metapedia in the extreme northern part of New Brunswick.

Its own tributary streams are famous for their fishing, such names as the Tobique, river and lake, and Temiscouata being again a sure guarantee of sport. The right of salmon fishing, on all the principal streams within the Provinces, is held by lessees under its federal or local governments. Permission to fish is usually granted to visitors by the lessees.

ON ST. JOHN RIVER

Such as are or become vacant are sold at public auction at Fredericton, the capital. Further information on this point can be obtained from the Crown Land Office, Fredericton.

The tourist-sportsman must not from this infer that he is debarred from angling in these waters. Though some are sold there are riparian privileges enough for all without trespass, and the angler is sure to receive a thoroughly honest welcome.

Above the Tobique numerous tributaries enter the St. John, which may be passed by the tourist, until Grand River, fourteen miles above the

Grand Falls, is reached. Its station and telegraph office is St. Leonard's. Grand River is not specially noted for its fishing, but is worthy of mention as a favorite way of reaching the Restigouche, the most famous of Canadian salmon rivers.

Next above St. Leonard's, and thirty-nine miles above Grand Falls, is Edmundston, the northern terminus of the New Brunswick Railway. It is prettily situated on rising ground at the confluence of the Madawaska and St. John. The little village boasts of little except its scenery, and the quaint customs and manners of its people. It contains a good hotel, and its chief claim to the sportsman's consideration is that it forms the headquarters for the great fishing trips to the upper St. John.

Madawaska, Green River and Fish River enter the St. John in this vicinity; the Madawaska from Lake Temisconata in the Province of Quebec; the Fish from Eagle Lakes in North Maine, and the Green from four lakes in Northern New Brunswick, which have not yet been supplied with names, but are termed 1st, 2d, 3d, and 4th. Possibly, the stock of names has run out among the myriad sheets of water which the section holds, and some future visitor may embalm his name or fancy forevermore by bestowing a cognomen upon these hidden lakes.

Upon all the tributaries of the St. John above Grand Falls good troutfishing may be enjoyed. At present, and until the projected government fishway is completed, salmon cannot ascend the falls. The ordinary means of locomotion employed by sportsmen upon the rivers and lakes of Northern New Brunswick is the log canoe or *peroigue*. This will carry three persons, including the guide, and the camping outfit. French guides can be procured for a dollar a day. They will furnish the canoes, blankets for their own use, plates, etc. The sportsman must provide his tent, his personal outfit, and his provisions.

Indian guides with bark canoes may be chosen at the visitor's option, or *batteaus* for larger parties. Good guides can be obtained at Andover, Grand Falls or Edmundston, without difficulty. It is not usually necessary to engage them in advance; but, if requested, the hotel-keepers at any of the towns will arrange it.

GRAND FALLS.

Although not partaking in an eminent degree in the title of fishing resort, we cannot leave the St. John's River without a reference to Grand Falls, which presents a variety of attractions in the grandeur of the cataract, the rugged sublimity of the gorge, the fury of the rapids, the rich coloring of the rocks, the lovely outlooks from its high hills, the charming drives, the strong pure air, the quaint customs of the French *habitans*, all combined to give the visitor pleasure.

The old town, settled, as were many of its neighbors, by remnants of the exiled Acadian band, after long wanderings, has ever been a point of interest to the traveller. Even in the old stage days, when the nearest railroad station was seventy-five miles distant, the Falls attracted many visitors. In situation the town is bounded upon three sides by the river, which here makes an abrupt bend encompassing the town, which stands upon a horseshoe peninsula thus formed. It is laid out with mathematical regularity, and with refreshing regard for elbow-room. Broadway — in name and nature — runs through the centre of the town; at one end is the railway station, and at the other the falls.

The river narrows as it reaches the cataract, and widens again to its original dimension immediately after its passage of the tortuous course around the town. On either hand its banks rise into steep bluffs, one hundred and twenty-five feet high upon the west, and two hundred and fifty feet descent from town to river upon the eastern side. The cataract itself exceeds the anticipation, its plunge is seventy-five feet, and the distance from one side of the gorge to the other, in a straight line, is three hundred feet. Except in very dry summers there is an unbroken curtain of water from bank to bank, falling into a whirlpool of terrific power. Clouds of spray are ever drifting up from the abyss, moved this way and that with listless motion. This ofttimes at night produces a lunar bow which spans the fall, and, occasionally, will-o'-the-wisps hover over the moist, mossy caverns.

Of course, the fall is not without its romance of the Indian Maiden. This time, so says tradition, it was a daughter of the Milicites taken prisoner by the Mohawks, their ancient enemy, who had killed her father and brothers. Her captor planned a night descent upon her tribe, and she was directed to build a fire to mark the nearest point to the falls which could be safely approached by canoes. She built the fire on the rocks below the falls, and then, as a guarantee of good faith, led the foremost canoe of the advance. Straight for the light she steered. Closely the warriors followed; over the falls the whole band sailed and none escaped.

The points of interest about Grand Falls, apart from the fall itself, are the Gorge, which is spanned by a suspension bridge affording a fine view down the Narrows, and "The Wells," within the Gorge, about midway between the Upper and Lower Basins. These wells are immense holes worn in the rock by the action of the water upon small stones. They occur in the vicinity of nearly all water-falls, but at the Grand Falls are exceptionally large. They form an interesting study to the geologist, as indeed do all the curious rock formations of the neighborhood.

There is much of interest hereabout which warrants a longer description, but we must journey eastward. Such, then, is the St. John, a river teeming with beauty and with sport, whose grand natural attractions are supplemented in a high degree by the allurements of its forests, lakes and streams; a river followed throughout almost its entire course by the New Brunswick Railway, and which is best and most advantageously reached by the ocean route from Boston, Portland or Passamaquoddy to St. John's City, thence direct by rail, or to a connection with the rail route at Fredericton by steamers of the "Union Line," plying the river daily between the seaport and capital.

Leaving St. John, by crossing the cantilever bridge, the train loses the river at Westfield, a few miles out, to find it again at Fredericton, the capital of New Brunswick, situated upon the St. John some eighty-five miles by the river from the sea, and sixty-six miles by rail.

Between the two cities the river is at its broadest and recalls an incident. During one old-time winter this long reach of water, then ice, was the scene of an interesting race between the teams of Lord North, who commanded the garrison at St. John, and Larry Stivers, a butcher of Fredericton, who had accepted his wager of £500. Possibly the leader of the British Rugulars found life a trifle dull in garrison at St. John after Crimean battles, and did this to stir up the monkeys for the time.

Be that as it may, the race was run, with honors easy until near the finish, when one of Larry's horses fell, and, before he could be cleared, Lord North secured a lead which brought him in ahead. North refused to accept the wager, but, striking the butcher's palm, exclaimed: "Keep it, Larry! You're the only man in the province with courage to run that race." So the story goes.

A steamboat line now plies the river through the scene of the North-Stivers struggle from St. John to Fredericton. The "Union Line" it is termed, and the visitor has to choose between it and the rail ride to Fredericton.

FREDERICTON is beautifully situated upon a level plain, directly upon the St. John River, with New Brunswick hills surrounding. It is a pretty place and well worth a visit. As capital of the province it contains the Parliament Buildings and the Government House, within fine grounds; a cathedral, normal school, and other structures of note, all tree-embowered by magnificent elms, planted with keen foresight by the city fathers of the past, to the enjoyment of the present generation.

Tall elms and flower gardens are Fredericton's specialties, to which must be added its suburban drives, which are numerous and very pleasing. One of these, "the old road," discloses such extensive and beautiful vistas of scenery, wherever a break in the dense foliage occurs, that many tourists pronounce it unsurpassed.

Leaving Fredericton, with its broad sweep of the river behind, we continue on through a series of inconsiderable towns to Woodstock Junction and Newburgh. From the latter point a branch connects for Houlton, Maine, through Woodstock, while we continue on in search of the famous salmon and trout streams of Northern New Brunswick.

After leaving the junction point at Newburgh, the road again strikes the St. John and follows it to its very head-waters. As the train skirts the river, which is in full view upon the left, it crosses numerous tributaries famous for their fishing, as the Tobique, and others, which approach the Southwest Miramichi and Restigouche. There is this peculiarity about the New Brunswick rivers, they approach each other by serpentine windings, and by the myriad arms of their affluents, until it is possible to visit with canoe and paddle a great section of country, by "carrying" across the narrow intervening space.

Thus, for example, one might leave the train of the New Brunswick Railway at Kent Station, and *ascend* the Shiktehawk, branch of the St. John, to its *almost* juncture with the northwest branch of the Miramichi, and from thence *descend* that river through its famous fishing and hunting-grounds, or, by a carry of two miles only, from the head of Salmon or Grand rivers ; other branches of the St. John reach the Restigouche itself.

The same is true, in reverse, by the route of the Intercolonial Railway from St. John. This road crosses the heads of the bays, outlets of the Miramichi, Restigouche, and a host of others of only lesser note, and inlets for the salmon which have given the streams their noble reputation.

From the bays one must now ascend these streams and carry to the affluents of the St. John. Both provincial lines of railway offer this peculiar facility to the sportsman. For hundreds of miles numerous rivers, navigable to canoe and paddle, intersect the roads, and the tourist has but to choose from the many streams, and with the stream its most convenient station.

To the sportsman then let us say : Here is a country of unlimited extent, which is open by such means as the above to anyone who can sit in a birch and ply a paddle ; here is game worthy of your rifle, and game-fish such as no other section of earth can boast.

To reach this *Ultima Thule*, the water route from Boston to St. John is named, as adding novelty to the rail-ride from St. John. For the purpose of guiding the sporting fraternity to this region, we enter in detail the fishing-waters of New Brunswick.

NEAR FREDERICTON.

HEAD HARBOR, CAMPOBELLO, N.B.

CHAPTER EIGHTH

THE SALMON STREAMS OF NEW BRUNSWICK AND HOW TO REACH THEM
— THE TOBIQUE, ITS LAKES AND MOUNTAINS —
A VIEW FROM BALD HEAD.

ONE excellent salmon stream, the Southwest Miramichi, is reached from Kent, a station one hundred and twenty-two miles from St. John on the New Brunswick Railway. Anglers can suit their fancy or convenience as to where they will procure their outfit. Those who have the necessary appliances for camping and sport will, of course, bring them, others can secure good outfits in St. John or Fredericton. Provisions for the trip should be purchased before leaving the towns for the forest. Sportsmen should bring their own tents if possible.

Teams can be secured at Kent Station, which will bear the sportsman and outfit to the river, distant but fifteen miles. From the point where the road from the station strikes the southwest branch to Boisetown — upon the main river — is sixty miles. From Boisetown the sportsman may choose the route by canoe and carry, or by road forty-five miles to Fredericton, or return the way he came.

The best salmon-hole is at Burnt Hill, about twenty-five miles down stream from the point of embarkation. Other favorite places are the Clearwater Rocky Bend, Rocky Brook, and Three-mile Rapids. The salmon are not as large as those taken on the Restigouche, rarely reaching above twenty-five pounds in weight, but they are gamy and afford fine sport. One who succeeds in landing a specimen need not fear to tackle a forty-pounder.

As an instance of the abundance of the fish in this stream comes the fact that twenty salmon have been taken by one angler in a single afternoon, while the same gentleman killed five full-grown salmon and hooked the sixth within an hour at the Rocky Bend.

The Miramichi takes its rise some two hundred miles or more from the sea, near the St. John and its tributaries, and drains an area equal to fully one quarter of the province. It is navigable from its mouth to large vessels for forty-six miles, and for canoes for many hundreds. It forms the grand sportsman's highway for reaching every quarter of a superb game region, where sport is unlimited amid moose, caribou, deer, bears, wolves, foxes, raccoons, loup-cerviers and all the smaller animals of the forest, while game-fish may be killed from the canoe in passage.

Both the New Brunswick and the Intercolonial railways offer routes, the first for reaching the headwaters of the tributary rivers to the Miramichi, and the latter crossing the parent stream, where, at its entrance to the great bay of the same name, are situated the towns of New Castle and Chatham. New Castle is a good point of departure for the upper river.

THE TOBIQUE.

Twenty miles above Kent Station the two New Brunswick towns of Perth and Andover lie upon opposite banks of the river St. John, and midway between enters the *Tobique*.

Andover, New Brunswick, a pretty rural village, is its railway and telegraph station. At Andover the sportsman should stop for a time to secure a guide and canoe. These can be hired at the Indian village, which stands just above the junction of the two streams.

This tributary of the St. John is named by travellers the most picturesque stream in America, while an additional attraction lies in the fact that it affords excellent fishing. It is a great spawning ground for salmon, and the trout in its waters are legion. From its mouth to Nictaux — the Forks — is about sixty-three miles. Here the river divides into three branches, each some fifty miles long, all meeting at the Forks in one deep pool, wherein one may see great salmon swimming, and the encircling trees cast their shadow and image upon the water.

The entrance to the Tobique from the St. John is tame, but a mile farther on perpendicular walls of rock raise their heads on either shore. Here occur "The Narrows," a striking bit of scenery. They are one-half mile long, from fifty to one hundred feet wide, the walls rising in some places one hundred to one hundred and fifty feet in height.

The river widens out above The Narrows, and in its windings presents a wonderful variety of scene. Twenty-eight miles above the St. John is the great Plaster Cliff, an enormous deposit of red sandstone. It has a frontage on the river for half a mile, and rises to a height of one hundred and thirty-five feet. The cliff presents the appearance of an enormous ruin as one's canoe floats by at night. Twelve miles farther on is Blue Mountain Bend. The Blue Mountains, upon the right in ascending, have an elevation of sixteen hundred feet above the sea, and add to the beauty of the Tobique. Ten miles above, Bald Head rises twenty-two hundred feet, and terminates in almost a complete cone, its summit having about half the area of an ordinary railway car. It can be ascended on its northern and western sides only; on the south and east it towers nearly perpendicularly for one thousand feet. It rises from a valley approached by a forest road, affording never-to-be-forgotten glimpses of its rugged summit.

Many sportsmen voyaging the Tobique leave the river to climb Bald Head, lured by the extended view obtainable from its summit, which includes in its far-reaching sweep one hundred miles of the winding course of the river, distant mountains, among them famous Katahdin in Northern Maine, and millions of acres of New Brunswick wilds.

The fishing thus far has been good in point of numbers, but the fish are not large. It is necessary to know where to angle, but the guides can tell you. The Indian guides of the Tobique are trusty fellows, strong and active in their canoes, wonderfully adept with the salmon-spear, and zealous for their patrons' comfort.

Famous fishing may be enjoyed about the Forks, while of the streams into which the river divides at this point the left-hand branch, called the Little Tobique, is best for trout. The right-hand branch, or Campbell River, is a favorite resort for salmon, while the Mamozekel, or central branch, is not remarkable for its fish.

It is a singular fact that salmon will only go to the right-hand branch, and white-fish only to the left-hand branch. One-half mile from Nictaux, on the left-hand branch, is the celebrated White-fish Hole. There is usually good trout fishing there.

From its forks following the deviating streams to the right and left, — no one ascends the central branch for sport, — brings one to the lakes which form the sources of the Tobique. Ascend the Little Tobique, — it is best for trout fishing — you will find its source in Little Tobique Lake, a pretty sheet of water noted for its big trout, between which and Lake Nepisiquit, the source of the river of same name, exists a carry of but three miles. The river Nepisiquit flows in an entirely opposite direction from the Tobique, and, crossing the Province, finds the sea in the Baie Des Chaleurs, an arm of the Gulf of St. Lawrence.

CHAPTER NINTH

TO THE NORTHERN PROVINCES AND THE FAR-FAMED RESTIGOUCHE — THE CLEAR WATERS OF THE METAPEDIA — PROVINCIAL GAME LAWS.

RETURNING once more to St. John as the distributing point for travel east and north, to the limits of the province of New Brunswick, to Nova Scotia, and to Prince Edward Island and the island of Cape Breton, the tourist now embarks upon the great steel highway of the Intercolonial Railway.

From St. John to Sussex, a distance of forty-four miles, the country bordering the line is well settled and abounds in beautiful villages. The Kennebaccasis River here flows close beside the tracks for several miles, the hills rising on the distant shore in picturesque beauty. As RIVERSIDE is reached, one of the finest racing waters on the continent is brought to view. This is the scene of many notable aquatic contests. Here it was that the renowned Paris and Tyne crews struggled for victory one autumn morning years ago, when James Renforth, champion oarsman of England, fell from the English boat, and was carried to the shore to die. ROTHESAY, nine miles above the city, contains many handsome villas, the summer houses of St. John business men and others. Their ornamental trees and carefully arranged grounds have a very pleasing effect. Next HAMPTON is in great repute as a summer resort with the people of St. John, and then SUSSEX, one of the rising towns of the province. Sussex is situated in the prolific Kennebaccasis Valley, and has some of the most famous of the New Brunswick farms. Some fair trout-fishing is to be had in this vicinity, as numerous lakes lie within easy distance from the village. PETITCODIAC and SALISBURY lead on to MONCTON, the centre from which the busy operations of the Intercolonial system are controlled. Moncton is essentially a railway town; it contains the general offices and the shops of the company, and has a population of about five thousand. Here is the Petitcodiac River, which empties into Shepody Bay, the very head of the Bay of Fundy; it is a continuation of the bay itself as far as Moncton, up which the waters of Fundy ascend with a "bore," which, to be more explicit, means an advancing wall of water six feet and more in height. This is worth seeing, and worth respecting, too, if you are out in a boat and don't know how to manage it. At Moncton diverging lines of rail reach Point Du Chene, whence steamers cross the Northumberland Straits to Prince Edward Island, while rail lines run down the great peninsula of Nova Scotia to Halifax, and other points which we shall reach later in description. Now, we journey northward over the long line of the Intercolonial Northern Division, which reaches Point Levi, opposite the ancient city of Quebec.

From Moncton to the Miramichi, the railway passes through a country which presents no particular attraction to the eye. It is so far from the shore that none of its flourishing settlements are seen. The traveller for this reason is apt to acquire a poor idea of the country. There is, however, a fine farming and fishing district all along the coast, and some large rivers of which the head waters only are crossed.

At NEWCASTLE the Miramichi River is crossed, and at Chatham Junction, passed just before reaching the river, a branch railway runs to Chatham-town, a few miles to the eastward.

One whose time is limited need not wander far from Chatham or Newcastle to find abundant sport. He is in a country whose annual export of salmon and bass is something incredible. Rod fishing may be had in any direction. There are, for special points, the Little Southwest and Renous rivers with their many lakes, some of which have never been fully explored. Wherever in these streams there exists a high bank upon one side and a low beach upon the other, will be found a pool in which salmon will be sure to resort. The Ox Bow, on the Little Southwest, is a favorite spot for anglers. The Main Northwest is a particularly good stream. These are branches of the *Miramichi*, a name which is synonymous with sport. Continue on to BATHURST, on the Baie Des Chaleurs ; this is one of the best laid out towns in the province, and a particularly pleasant spot, both for residents and visitors. There are numerous pleasant drives following river roads, taking in the falls of the Tete-a-Gauche or Fairy River, three miles from town, and the rough waters of the Nepisiquit on the return. For falls, however, there is nothing in the vicinity to equal the Grand Falls of the Nepisiquit, twenty-one miles distant. There are two pitches, the total descent being 105 feet, and the grandeur of the rocky heights by which the river is overlooked requires a personal inspection to form a true conception of the scene.

This is a great region for salmon and trout. The former are taken in the Nepisiquit as far as the Grand Falls. At the Rough Water, three miles from Bathurst, they are particularly plenty, but good pools may be found all along the river ; caribou and bears abound in the forest and plains through which we have come from Newcastle to Bathurst. Partridges are plenty in all parts of the country, and fly across the path of the traveller on every highway. The country is wild enough to suit all purposes of sport; you can drop a line in any stream and something will rise to it, while skill with the rifle will bring proud trophies from these forest retreats. Guides are easily obtained in all this immense preserve, and are reliable men, who add much to the pleasure of the outing, relieving the sportsman of all care of the camp and equipage, as well as pointing out to their patron the favorite haunts of game. Much the same aspect of country is presented from Bathurst northward, excepting that in all the distance one obtains amphibious glances of the sea as

ON THE RESTIGOUCHE.

the rails skirt the shore of the great Baie Des Chaleurs. This far northern inlet from the Gulf of St. Lawrence is ninety miles long, from fifteen to twenty miles broad, and bears neither rock nor hindrance to the safe passage of the largest ships. It presents a famous yachting course, and is renowned for its salt water fishing; all of the numerous rivers which flow into the bay are good fishing streams; sea trout abound in the estuaries and brook trout in the waters above *The Restigouche* and *Metapedia*. But it is at the head of this bay, the Baie Des Chaleurs, that the grand culmination of salmon streams is reached in the Restigouche and Metapedia, names which are graven deep upon the hearts of all true anglers. Here huge forty-pound salmon lurk to test the sportsman's skill. It was a Restigouche salmon which tipped the scale at fifty-four pounds, and numbers have been caught weighing forty-eight pounds each. Salmon fishing commences about the middle of May, and all the rivers abound with the great and glorious fish.

At Metapedia Station, on the Intercolonial, the Restigouche is crossed by the trains where the river is spanned by a beautiful railway bridge, over one thousand feet in length. In the flat-iron caused by the junction of the two rivers, Metapedia and Restigouche, which interesting event occurs just below the station, stands the club-house of the Restigouche Salmon Club, a most advantageous site.

Never were better facilities offered for the thorough enjoyment of sport than here, and hundreds of Anglers and Knights of the Rifle annually enjoy the hospitality of the club-houses, if they are unfortunate in not being club-members themselves. The house is close beside the railway station, its broad veranda fronting to the same as if to welcome the coming and speed the parting guest.

Should one wish for the ideal wilderness, let him ascend this great river to its source, some two hundred miles away, or retire through some of its tributary arteries into the wilds of New Brunswick, hunting, fishing and camping, to their meeting with other offshoots of the Tobique or St. John.

THE "PORTAGE." HEADWATERS OF THE RESTIGOUCHE.

The Restigouche forms part way the boundary between the Provinces of New Brunswick and Quebec. The river's course is most erratic, and with its arms produces, on paper, the appearance of a many limbed tree trunk, but then, the same is characteristic of all rivers in these provinces. Numerous lakes, as the Temiscouata and Squatook, may be reached through these forest avenues, — indeed, the by-paths are innumerable, as streams run in every direction. All of them are safe for canoe navigation, so safe, indeed, that ladies with proper escort have ascended the St. John, crossed the narrow carry to the Restigouche and reverse.

METAPEDIA: LAKE AND RIVER.

A beautiful sheet of water is Lake Metapedia, the noblest sheet of inland water along the route. It lies among the highlands which border the River St. Lawrence, is sixteen miles in length and in parts reaches a width of five miles. Upon its clear waters the canoe of the sportsman glides through scenes elysian. Embosomed on its surface are islands rich in verdure, while the shores are luxuriantly decked with summer foliage.

The outlet of the lake is the famous Metapedia River, winding its way in graceful curves through its rich valley to the meeting with the Restigouche, and then the sea.

If the clear waters of the lake were — and they justly are — noted for their salmon, so too the river partakes of the honors. It has 222 rapids, great and small, fierce and wild, or gently rippling over beds of shining gravel. Salmon of the largest size are numerous, and here and there lurk those abnormally large fish, the killing of which with light fly-rod requires so much of skill and endurance, a pleasure long drawn out.

Space forbids our devoting too much of that valued article to the hunting and fishing resorts of New Brunswick, in a description which is to include the whole eastern country from St. John to the Atlantic. Consequently, with a few pointers concerning the game laws and restrictions required by the Provincial Government, we shall leave what remains for the tourist to find for himself.

The regulations of the department allow of fly fishing for salmon from the 30th of April to the 31st of August in Quebec, and from the 1st of March to the 15th of September in New Brunswick. In Nova Scotia (which we shall consider later, but not make a specialty of its fishing and hunting, preferring to generalize here) the best salmon rivers are on the Atlantic coast, though some which were formerly good have been "fished-out," or obstructed by dams. Where *good* fish-ways have been put in, the streams are not injured, but some of the old ways seem adapted for almost any purpose rather than the passage of salmon. One river, which does not empty on the Atlantic coast, deserves mention. It is the Shubenacadie, on which some fine sport has been had, and will doubtless be had in the future. Salmon cannot be fished for in the rivers to the westward of Halifax between the 31st of July and the 1st of March, nor in the other rivers between the 15th of August and the 1st of March. None of the rivers of Nova Scotia are leased.

Trout are abundant in all the lakes, rivers and estuaries along the line of railway, and the fishing is a free one. The close season is from the 1st of October to the 1st of January. The sea trout found in the estuaries are fine fish, and, though abundant in very many places, they are found in their perfection in the Tabusintac and Escuminac. They are greedy biters, and, it is said, will take almost any kind of fly. The arms of the sea are numerous estuaries on the Atlantic coast of Nova Scotia, are particularly good places for these fish, which find their feeding-grounds among the sand flats and the bars and among the beds of sea-weed in shoal water. June and July are the best months for seeking

them, though they may be found at all seasons. They are a very gamy fish, handsome in appearance and excellent eating.

PROVINCIAL GAME LAWS.

The Lower Provinces afford the best opportunities for moose and caribou hunting. The country lying back of the rivers on the northeast shore of New Brunswick, and the forests of Cumberland, Colchester, Halifax and Guysboro, in Nova Scotia, will give all the sport desired. Moose may now be killed in the Province of Quebec, after a long prohibitory season which came off September 1, 1888. The close season now is from the 1st of February to the 1st of September. Caribou can also be killed in Quebec, and the season is the one last mentioned. The penalty for violation is from $5 to $20. The close season for partridge is from the 1st of January to the 15th of September; for woodcock, snipe, etc., from the 1st of February to the 1st of September; and for geese and ducks from the 15th of April to the 1st of September. An hour before and after sunset are also set apart for the protection of snipe, woodcock, ducks and geese. Non-residents are required to take out a hunting license, the cost of which is $20, and the penalty for the non-compliance is double the amount of the fee.

In New Brunswick, the close season for moose, caribou and deer is from the 1st of February to the 1st of August. The penalty is a fine of from $10 to $60. Hunting with dogs is forbidden, under a penalty of $20, and any person may kill dogs which are chasing, or can be proved to have chased, such game. Three moose, five caribou or five deer, are allowed to be killed by each party in any one season. The flesh of such game must be carried out of the woods within ten days after the killing, with the exception of such as is killed during the latter part of December, when the flesh must be carried out within the first five days of January. The close season for partridge is from the 1st of March to the 20th of September; for woodcock and snipe, to the 14th of August. Non-residents are required to take out a license, the cost of which is the same as in Quebec.

In Nova Scotia the close season for moose and caribou is from the 1st of February to the 15th of September. No one person is allowed to take more than two moose and four caribou in any one year or season. The flesh is to be carried out of the woods within ten days after killing, and game killed during the latter part of January shall be carried out during the first five days of February. The penalty for the violation of these provisions is from $30 to $50, and a fine of $25 is imposed for hunting with dogs. The close season for partridge is between the first days of January and October, and that of woodcock, snipe and teal between the first days of March and August. Woodcock must not be killed before sunrise or after sunset. Blue-winged duck must not be taken between the first days of April and August. The annual licenses for non-residents expire on the 1st of August. They cost $30 each.

The foregoing are some of the provisions of the Game Laws of the three provinces. There are other provisions, in regard to trapping, using nets for wild fowl, hunting with artificial lights, etc., but as no sportsman will resort to such practices, these provisions need not be quoted.

CHAPTER TENTH

PRINCE EDWARD ISLAND AND CAPE BRETON — THE GARDEN OF THE
MARITIME PROVINCES — THE BRAS D'OR LAKES —
A RELIC OF THE LAST CENTURY.

THE tourist, if in New Brunswick, taking the morning train from St. John arrives at Point du Chene about noon, and steps from the train at the end of the Government Wharf right on board the fine twin-screw steamer " Northumberland," where a good dinner is always ready. By the time this is partaken of, the noble vessel slips out from the wharf and speedily takes her way to Summerside, a distance of some forty miles.

During the summer months the gulf is generally as smooth as a mill pond, and the good ship, as she glides through the water at the rate of seventeen miles an hour, scarce makes a motion to remind even the most sensitive to seasickness that their enemy is likely to visit them. Some amuse themselves with music, and a suspicion of amateurs generally fill the air with pieces rendered on the piano in the saloon, whilst the majority sit out on the deck watching the French settlements in New Brunswick as they are rapidly passed from Shediac to Cape Bauld. As this landmark and its church fade from view, Egmont Bay and Cape, on Prince Edward Island, with the green fields dotted with white houses, become distinct, Miscouche village and church on the highest land shows up nicely cut out on the sky line, while ahead the spires and buildings of Summerside grow nearer and nearer. A few minutes more and the lighthouse, built out on an iron caisson at the entrance of the harbor, is passed, and, moving somewhat more slowly, with the wharves and thickly clustered houses of Summerside on the one side and the Island Park and Hotel on the other, the steamer reaches the railway wharf, and the train is found waiting for the passengers. In a few minutes " All on board for Charlottetown " is heard, and all who had not arranged to stay in Summerside are whirling away through the greenest of green fields towards their destination.

Charlottetown covers a large space of land for its sixteen thousand inhabitants. The streets are straight and wide. There are several large squares kept open for the public, which have been planted with shade trees, flowers and shrubs, and laid out with nice walks and fountains. Queen Square — the largest — occupies a fine situation, and with its public buildings forming a line through its longest centre makes a fine appearance. In the centre is the Old Provincial Building of grey sandstone, flanked on either side,— east the Law Courts, a fine red brick building,

A Vacation Day.

and on the west by the Dominion Post-Office, etc. etc. Further west comes the Market House, with its large hall above, and on the east of the Law Courts the old church of St. Paul's, situated in its green field, with the red sandstone parsonage (a proof of the suitability of the Island stone for building purposes) and the large schoolhouse behind it, both on the southern side of the church. Around the square the best of the stores are found, many of them as fine brick or stone buildings as can be found in any city of the same size.

These with the Y. M. C. A., Zion Church, Banks and St. Patrick's School pretty well fill two sides of the large square, the rest being with few exceptions smaller wooden buildings of older date, soon to be supplanted by the more lasting brick structures which are rapidly growing in favor.

The upper part of the town is mostly devoted to private residences, many of which are large and ornate and mostly placed in flower gardens with ornamental shrubbery, which give an air of comfort and refinement which is easily recognized.

But until the tourist or pleasure-seeker has driven over the country roads of P. E. Island and strolled along its smooth, sandy shores, tracked up its little rivulets and seen the farms as they are, he cannot say he has seen P. E. I. They may have watched its shores from the deck of a steamer, admired the deep green of the cultivated fields, and wondered at the numerous buildings and its many churches in which its fifty-four people to the mile live and worship ; but until he has travelled behind a good horse in a comfortable carriage over the hills, one after the other in every direction, he cannot form a correct opinion of what this little patch of new red sandstone thrust out into the gulf away from its older sisters really is. Small it undoubtedly is, but one hundred and thirty-one miles long, with a width from two miles at Summerside to thirty-five miles in others, and containing one and a quarter million acres, is large enough to support its present one hundred and ten thousand inhabitants and send away vast quantities of agricultural produce to the Maritime Provinces of Canada and the United States.

So much for the country ; now, what are its attractions as a summer resort?

A cool, invigorating atmosphere, the sea breezes passing over it from every quarter. The best of sea bathing, either in the smooth waters of the numerous harbors or amidst the rollers of the north shore.

Boating in harbors or open gulf; sea and river fishing, of which mackerel and trout give the best sport.

For shooting, plover, snipe, wild duck, rabbits, partridge, and that king of game — woodcock.

Then for driving, riding, or the use of the bicycle, the island roads are smooth, free from stones and not too hilly ; and an ever changing, fresh looking country where no burnt-up grass lands or dreary stretches of barren, stony land mar the scene.

Summerside, the western mart of the island, has grown up from the traffic with Point du Chene, and also enjoys quite a foreign trade, its enterprising merchants looking far and wide for markets new.

The population is about three thousand. It is situated amidst the very finest farming lands of the Province, and has within a few miles a number of thriving villages and settlements.

Daily communication to and from the mainland, from both Charlotte-town and Summerside, by steamer makes access and egress easy, whilst telegraph, telephone and post-offices are to be found in every settlement or village of any size, so that the tired business man to whom rest and health are the annual summer requirements may keep full communication with the outer world, and find P. E. Island a more restful retreat than the places so often chosen, and where multitudes gather and where cost of living and incentives to spend money almost equal city life.

CAPE BRETON ISLAND.

This is the point to which we have been leading, a country vying in interest with the last, and eminently worthy of a place beside it in this chapter.

From New Glasgow a rail line called the Eastern Extension, which name, by the way, is no misnomer, runs to Port Mulgrave on the famous Strait of Canso. It is a short run, some ninety miles at best from the Pictou Wharf to Pirates Harbor on the Strait, through Antigonish, called the prettiest village in Eastern Nova Scotia. Its neat, tidy buildings stand amid beautiful shade trees, — and then its people! If you want to find a type of able-bodied men, make your selection at random from the brawny Scots who go to make up the population of Eastern Nova Scotia, and especially Antigonish.

The word Antigonish means Big Fish River; the fishing, however, does not warrant the title. There are other towns passed by the traveller *en route* to Cape Breton but none which call for special remark, except Tracadie, where there is a splendid view of the gulf. Here also is a Trappist Monastery and an Indian Reservation.

After leaving Tracadie the train steams down the narrowing shores of Nova Scotia to the Strait of Canso — or Canseau — and the through passengers are taken by the train to Port Mulgrave, the deep water terminus, to embark upon the boat for the Island of Cape Breton.

This narrow strait, some fourteen miles long and one mile in width, forms the great highway between the Gulf of St. Lawrence and the Atlantic. As a natural consequence when the extensive commerce between the two is narrowed down to these confining walls, the waters of the strait are thronged by steam and sail, adding to the natural beauty of the spot the charm of breezy life, — an animated picture. The passage of Canso is soon made, and Port Hawkesbury reached, upon the Cape Breton side. Here the traveller can take steamer, which makes daily connections with trains, and lands passengers at the head of East Bay, ten miles from Sydney at the eastern extremity of the island, through the celebrated Bras D'Or — *The Arm of Gold*.

This imprisoned sea, one hundred miles long and from ten rods to ten miles wide, divides the island of Cape Breton into two parts. For about fifty miles its waters are sheltered from the ocean, of which it forms a part, and in this length it expands into bays, inlets and romantic havens, with islands, peninsulas, and broken lines of coast, combining all to please.

High mountains and cliffs tower above the lake on every hand, at many points rising sheer from the water, casting their shadows down through the clear depths ; again rising in the distance, and with intervening fertile valleys between it and the lake, showing the white cottages of the farming and fisher folks who make home of this far eastern country.

Cape Breton is rich in geological wonders. Its coal deposits, which underlie much of the island, and are supposed to extend in one continuous vein one hundred and fifty miles long to the mines of Pictou, in Nova Scotia, are inexhaustible, and crop out in divers out-of-the-way places. Dig a few feet below the surface in almost any place upon the island and your reward will be a rich seam of coal. Many families have a natural coal bin in the cellar, provided when the continent was making. Fossils rare and curious are common upon the shores of Cape Breton in the coal strata, and wrenched therefrom by the sea. The professor might secure a wonderful addition to his cabinet from this vicinity.

BRAS D'OR LAKE.

In the passage of the Bras D'Or another notable geological formation is brought to view, where far off to the eastward glisten in the sunlight the heights of the Marble Mountain. Its product is a very fair white marble, which has not been extensively quarried, coal being more in the line of trade.

We pass through the Bras D'Or to the towns which lie upon the seaward side of the isle. They are Sydney-old-town, noted for its coal mines, whose vast sunless depths extend for two miles under the ocean, and for its fine piers, from which are shipped annually immense quantities of Sydney coal, known wherever coal is burned, from the field which is estimated to contain a thousand million tons, not to include seams less than four feet in thickness, nor the vast quantities which lie under the sea between the islands of Cape Breton and Newfoundland. North Sydney is of more commercial importance than the old town. Within its harbor gather vessels of every class. It is a famous coaling station for ocean steamers, and a right lively little port.

Between Cape North and Cape St. Lawrence, upon the far northern extremity of the island, an ocean cable is landed in Aspy Bay and operated at North Sydney. It is but fifty miles from the North Cape to the Magdelen Islands, the cruising ground of the cod-fishing fleet to the Grand Banks of Newfoundland. Baddeck is another famous old town at the head of Ste. Ann's Bay, reached by steamer from Sydney. A few hours' journey from Baddeck will take one into a country where moose and caribou are plenty, and where the sportsman may either camp-out in the wilderness, or make his headquarters with some one of the well-to-do farmers of Inverness or Victoria county's occasional settlements.

THE RUINS OF LOUISBURG.

South of, and reached by narrow-gauge rail from Sydney, is Louisburg, on the Atlantic shore, where, upon the maps, it presents the appearance of being ever ready to drop off into space.

The Louisburg of to-day has a population of about one thousand souls, and is situated just across the harbor from the old fortified town which bears so important a part in history. The railroad fare from Sydney is but 75 cents, and all visitors to the island of Cape Breton should make the trip. The Louisburg Land Company's hotel affords fine accommodations, and the site of old Louisburg may be easily reached and the lines of its old fortifications traced.

Nearly a century has elapsed since the fall of Louisburg, and nothing remains to mark this stronghold of the French in America save the relics of a structure which cost the treasury of Louis XV. thirty millions of livres, and the labor of twenty-five years to erect. Its walls of stone, which made a circuit of two and one half miles, were thirty-six feet in height, and of a uniform thickness of forty feet. Fifteen thousand people were gathered in and about these walls; six thousand troops were locked within this fortress when the gate-key turned in the mammoth lock.

The foundations of the town were laid in the early part of the last century, just after the death of Louis XIV., and named in honor of the departed monarch. Nova Scotia proper had been granted here and there to adventurous would-be colonists and their leaders, but the ancient island Cape Breton still owed allegiance to the lilies of France. Of all the harbors which the island bore, this was selected as the most advantageous, and here was built the city which was designed to be the key to the Western Hemisphere.

"It was environed," says Belknap, "two miles and a half in circumference, with a rampart of stone from thirty to thirty-six feet high, and a ditch eight feet wide. There were six bastions and batteries, containing embrasures for one hundred and forty-eight cannon. On an island at the entrance of the harbor was planted a battery of thirty cannon, carrying twenty-eight-pound shot, and at the bottom of the harbor was a grand, or royal battery, of twenty-eight cannon, forty-two pounders, and two eighteen pounders. On a high cliff opposite the island-battery stood a lighthouse, and within this point, secure from all winds, was a careening wharf and a magazine of naval stores."

The entrance to the town was over a drawbridge, spanning the moat, near which was a circular battery mounting sixteen fourteen-pounder guns, and yet, with all their show of arms, Louisburg, the naval depot of France in America, the nucleus of its military power, the protector of its fisheries, the Sebastopol of the New World, fell before the undisciplined troops of the colonies of Massachusetts, Connecticut and New Hampshire, led by William Pepperel, a fish and shingle merchant of Maine.

In three years after its capture by the colonial troops Louisburg was restored to the French by the treaty of Aix-la-Chapelle. Ten years passed and a greater fleet, a more numerous army and heavier armament besieged its almost impregnable walls, when, in 1758, the English under Amherst, Boscawen and Wolfe gathered no less than twenty-three ships of war, eighteen frigates, and sixteen thousand land forces, with a proportionable train of cannons and mortars, against the city. It fell after a two months' storm of fire and iron, of rocket, shot, and shell — fell, and the lilies of France waved over Louisburg no more.

Possessed a second time of the fortress city, and the conquest of Canada achieved, England's edict went forth that Louisburg should be destroyed. It required two years and the aid of gunpowder to complete the work of demolition, but in the end it was thoroughly done and the

CLIFFS NEAR GRAND NARROWS

once proud city, which had borne a monarch's title, sank into a shapeless ruin.

To-day, the tourist stands amid the theatre of such events and with his opened history marks the scene of struggle. Here lay the frigates of Louis; opposite, where the parapets of stone are yet visible, was the grand battery of forty guns. There the great seventy-four blew up. This ground has shuddered day and night for continued weeks at the roar of battle; and here are we, summer travellers from the busy marts of trade, day-dreaming in this bit of Europe in America.

Prince Edward's Island and Cape Breton together form an attractive page in the summer literature of the Northeast. Many of their points and features must necessarily be omitted in the brief chapter devoted to them in the descriptive of the whole Maritime Provinces; and it is with the hope that the little which has been said will create a desire for a personal visit, that we leave their island shores for the lower peninsula of Nova Scotia.

POINT LEPREAUX LIGHT.

CHAPTER ELEVENTH

THE LOWER PENINSULA OF NOVA SCOTIA — HALIFAX, THE METROPOLIS
OF THE PROVINCE AND ITS FORTIFICATIONS — THE
ANNAPOLIS VALLEY — YARMOUTH.

TO REACH Halifax, and through it the "Land of Evangeline," by the rail-route, we take the diverging line from Truro, which has before been referred to as tipping abruptly down the peninsula of Nova Scotia, and follow through fertile fields and upland intervale, a transition, indeed, from the rugged scenery of Cape Breton, until this fine farming district is lost amid the desolate rocks which abound, to the exclusion of all other crops, at Windsor Junction, fourteen miles from Halifax.

At this point the Windsor and Annapolis Railway forms a junction with the Intercolonial, and "all change" for the run down the Annapolis Valley to Annapolis, on the famous "Basin." It is twelve miles by steamer through the Basin to Digby, where another line, the Western Counties Railway, leads to Yarmouth at the extreme of the peninsula, and the veritable jumping-off place of oft quotation.

Both the Windsor and Annapolis and Western Counties roads skirt the Bay of Fundy shore of Nova Scotia, linking its towns to the exclusion of the Atlantic coast line, which has its only railway point in Halifax. After leaving Windsor Junction the approach to the city of Halifax is along the shores of the famous Bedford Basin, upon which the city is situated — a noble marine view which deepens in interest as the train nears the journey's end.

Halifax, from the very nature of its position, the most eastern city of its size upon the Western Hemisphere, is, in name, familiar to all Americans, and is oftener in the mouths of man, — as a mild sort of invective, — than many a Western metropolis.

One could go farther, however, and fare worse than being consigned to Halifax, for this is the most thoroughly British city on the continent, and, as such, holds much of interest to the American tourist. It is a garrison town as well as a naval station, and one meets in the streets the regulation Red-Coats and Blue-Jackets at every turn. Everything suggesting impending hostilities, "the pomp and circumstance of glorious war," encounters the peaceful tourist upon street-corners, while the citadel towers upon the summit of the hill-city of Halifax.

Let us climb this hill, and from the great stone fortress look out over the broad bay 256 feet below.

Like nearly all large cities upon the seaboard, the site of Halifax is a peninsula, with the sea upon the east and west. To the south and east is the harbor, which narrows as it reaches the upper end of the city and expands again into Bedford Basin, which affords ten miles of safe anchorage. The approach to the city is strongly fortified, as well becomes this British stronghold.

View from the citadel the magnificent bay, where vessels, flying every flag which protects a floating commerce, are at anchor. Let your vision extend over the islands to the wide ocean beyond, bounded only by the horizon's line. Turn to the scene presented inland, where stretch away vast verdant plains dotted with settlements and cottages, with now and then glimpses of blue water, and you will return to the town below, fairly impressed with Halifax and its surroundings.

The fortifications upon McNab's and George's Islands, as well as the various forts around the shore, are all well worth a visit after the citadel. Visitors are readily allowed to inspect the works, but sketches or pencil notes of the defences will not be permitted by the authorities. After a visit the tourist will have no doubts of the exceeding strength of Halifax over all the cities of America.

Hospitality is a virtue particularly grateful to the stranger tourist, and hospitality abounds among the good people of Halifax, even for the rebellious Yankee, in spite of the Loyalist forefathers of the city. The hotels afford fine accommodations, with plenty of solid accompaniments —the viands of Merry England, specialties partaken of so generously by the characters of Dickens — which give an appetite on the reading merely of those delightful spreads — washed down by generous portions of right good H'inglish H'ale.

Livery outfits, for the many delightful drives out and about the city, are procurable at modest rates of hire, and boats of every description for the exploration of the Bedford Basin may always be had.

There is much to be seen inside the city. The Province Buildings, new and old; the Museum, the Public Gardens, the Fish-Market, and the many public institutions, all open to inspection and all worthy a visit. Halifax has direct rail and steamship connection for all parts of the world, and marks the point of shortest ocean passage between America and Europe. It is the port of call for many lines crossing the Atlantic, and without delay one may go to Liverpool, Glasgow, the West Indies, New York, Boston, Portland, Newfoundland, or Quebec. If you desire a sea voyage, choose!

THE PENINSULA OF NOVA SCOTIA.

Bordering the Atlantic, from Yarmouth upon the south to Halifax in the centre and beyond to the Strait of Canso, a rugged coast line with deep bays, numerous peninsulas and islands, receives the almost mid-ocean waves. It is a wild shore, where fishing is extensively carried on, the numerous arms of the sea admirably suiting the occupation of the people. These coast settlements are linked with Halifax by water-routes; the rail is yet to come.

Back from the coast line the country abounds with heavy forests, and is abundantly watered by lakes and streams. Moose and caribou roam these forest wilds, and may be found within easy distance from the settlements. The fishing is excellent, and from June to September the catch of sea trout and salmon cannot fail to satisfy all.

PARTRIDGE ISLAND, ENTRANCE TO ST. JOHN HARBOR.

CHAPTER TWELFTH

BAY OF FUNDY S.S. CO. TO DIGBY, ANNAPOLIS, AND THE LAND OF EVANGELINE — THE END OF GRAND PRÉ.

THE short route to the Garden of the Provinces — the Annapolis Valley — is via the Steamer Monticello (running in connection with the route we have been following), which leaves St. John at 7.30 A. M. daily, Sunday excepted, crossing the Bay of Fundy to Annapolis and Digby, there to meet trains of the Windsor and Annapolis and the Western Counties railways running north and south on the peninsula.

The City of Monticello is a first-class side-wheel steamer, finely fitted and furnished, combining luxury and comfort obtainable only on this class of steamboats.

The passage of the steamer from the Bay of Fundy into the Annapolis Basin is through the narrow Digby Strait, with a range of high hills upon either side. The whole coast from Brier Island, at the southern entrance of the Bay of Fundy, to Blomidon on the Basin of Minas, a distance of one hundred and thirty miles, is protected by these rocky barriers, which here divide in a narrow waterway. After passing the strait this arm of the sea broadens into the great land-locked basin. The first stop of the steamer is at Digby, then on to Annapolis, twelve miles distant, and about midway the beautiful inland sea. The steamboat journey between the two towns is full of interest.

ANNAPOLIS ROYAL.

This is the oldest European settlement in America, north of the Gulf of Mexico. It was the ancient capital of Acadia. We have noted it before as the first landing place of the Des Monts expedition in 1604, who afterward visited Passamaquoddy, passing the luckless winter on Douchet's Island in the St. Croix. The town was then Port Royal; changed a century later, after the English conquest, to Annapolis in honor of their queen. The early settlement was farther down shore than the present town, but all about is historic ground. Where now all is peace and beauty, the blast of war's great organs rent the sky, in the early days of conquest, when the roses of England supplanted the lilies of France in the possession of these shores. Port Royal has shared the fate of Louisburg and other Acadian strongholds, and its fort has become a ruin.

It is here, at Annapolis, that we take the train through "the Valley," to the historic ground about the Basin of Minas. A valley, indeed, and in every sense of the word. It lies between the South Mountain range and the North Mountains which guard the coast line. Along its entire length and directly through its centre extend the rails of the Windsor and Annapolis Railway, for mile after mile passing vast orchards, white with apple blossoms, or laden with tempting fruit. The finest of orchards, fair farms, and fertile fields stretching away to the mountain borders. Such is the landscape. The air is fragrant with growing crops, and the eye never wearies with the charmingly rural scene.

BLOMIDON, N. S.

At the farther end of the valley, seventy miles from Annapolis, lies the tragic theatre of events which has given us Evangeline. Here are the idyllic meadows of Grand Pré, protected from the sea by dikes, erected by the sturdy French peasantry of long ago. Yonder Blomidon rises from the sea, silent guardian over the Basin of Minas, which curving inland, one magnificent crescent of sixty miles depth, bathes the Grand Prairies of Acadian Land. Here lived and loved, one hundred and fifty years ago, a simple people in a state of rural felicity which seems inconsistent with the frailties and passions of human nature. Among them real misery was unknown, and benevolence anticipated the demands of poverty. Every misfortune was relieved before it could be felt, without ostentation and without meanness. It was a society of brethren, every individual of which was ready to give, and to receive, what he thought the common right of mankind. In 1755 the colony numbered a population of eighteen thousand souls.

Here, at the Gaspereau's mouth, on the shores of the Basin of Minas, was situated the village of Grand Pré. Ascend some one of the many elevations of the Gaspereau and look to-day upon the scene.

A summer pastoral, rich meadow lands, dikes in the distance, and detached cottages in place of the hundreds of thatched roofs which once covered the exiled Acadians. Few traces remain of the old French village; the dikes still shut out the sea, and the road taken by the exiles on their sad way to the King's ships may still be followed by the tourist; other than this —

"Not but tradition remains, of the beautiful village of Grand Pré."

Assuming that the reader is by this time surfeited with description of sea and shore, highland and lowland scenery, which must at best employ many stereotyped phrases, let us escape for a time to relate

PETIT MANAN LIGHT.

THE STORY OF THE ACADIANS.

By the treaty of Aix La Chapelle, Cape Breton was ceded to the French and Nova Scotia to the English. The French colonists in the Annapolis Valley had taken the oath of fidelity to the English Crown, but they refused to take the oath of allegiance which forced them to bear arms against their countrymen and the Indians, who had always been their firm friends.

This stand was particularly distasteful to the English colonists of New England and Nova Scotia who were engaged in the fierce border wars with the allied French and Indians, and their "sullen neutrality" was considered just cause of offence.

Accordingly, a new oath of allegiance was tendered by King George II., by which all Acadians were required to become loyal subjects of the British Crown, and as such to bear arms against the allied forces of countrymen and friends.

The people revolted, and three hundred of the younger and braver among them took up arms against their oppressors. At the fort of Beau Séjour the little band made their gallant stand, and were defeated. In vain the majority protested that this act of the few was contrary to their wishes, contrary to their peaceful habits, and beyond their control. The whole Acadian people were by this rash act placed under the ban.

The edict went forth. All were to be transported from their homes and fertile fields, banished, dispersed among the various British colonies to the south. To carry out this plan, five transports and a force of New England troops were dispatched to the Basin of Minas. Arrived there a proclamation, so ambiguous in its nature as to give no hint of its object, was issued to the people of the district of Grand Pré; it read as follows:—

To the inhabitants of the District of Grand Pré, Minas, River Canard, etc., as well ancient, as young men and lads:

"Whereas, his Excellency, the Governor, has instructed us of his late resolution, respecting the matter proposed to the inhabitants, and has ordered us to communicate the same in person, his Excellency being desirous that each of them should be fully satisfied of his Majesty's intentions, which he has also ordered us to communicate to you, such as they have been given to him. We therefore order and strictly enjoin, by these presents, all of the inhabitants, as well of the above-named District, as of all other districts, both old men and young men, as well as all the lads of ten years of age, to attend at the church of Grand Pré on Friday, the fifth instant, at three of the clock in the afternoon, that we may impart to them what we are ordered to communicate to them,

declaring that no excuse will be admitted on any pretense whatever, on pain of forfeiting goods and chattels, in default of real estate. Given at Grand Pré, second of September, 1755, and twenty-ninth of his Majesty's reign.   JOHN WINSLOW,
Colonel Commanding."

Four hundred and eighteen able-bodied men heeded the summons. These were shut into the church, and Colonel Winslow, placing himself with his officers in the centre, addressed them.

You have read the remainder in Longfellow's version of the tale. The poor people, unconscious of any crime, petitioned Colonel Winslow for leave to visit their families, and entreated him to detain a part only of the prisoners as hostages, urging with tears and prayers their intention to fulfill their promise of returning after taking leave of their kindred and consoling them in their distress and misfortune. The answer of Colonel Winslow to this petition was to grant leave of absence to twenty only for a single day. This sentence they bore with fortitude and resignation, but when the hour of embarkation arrived, in which they were to part with their friends and relatives without a hope of ever seeing them again, and to be dispersed among strangers, whose language, customs, and religion were opposed to their own, the weakness of their human nature prevailed, and they were overpowered with a sense of their miseries. The young men were first ordered to go on board one of the vessels. This they instantly and peremptorily refused to do, declaring that they would not leave their parents, but expressing a willingness to comply with the order, provided they were permitted to embark with their families. The request was rejected, and the troops ordered to fix bayonets and advance toward the prisoners, a motion which had the effect of producing obedience on the part of the young men, who forthwith commenced their march. The road from the chapel to the shore — just one mile in length — was crowded with women and children, who, on their knees, greeted them as they passed with their tears and their blessings, while the prisoners advanced with slow and reluctant steps, weeping, praying, and singing hymns. This detachment was followed by the seniors, who passed through the same scene of sorrow and distress. In this manner was the whole male part of the population of the District of Minas put on board the five transports stationed in the river Gaspereau, and thus were the remainder of the 18,000 Acadians sent into a similar exile. Who has not followed them in fancy, and through the beautiful verse of Evangeline.

Turn now to a more pleasing subject, the beautiful valley which they left. The author of "Sparrowgrass Papers"—old-timers will remember them with pleasure — says in description of the Maritime Provinces :

"Much as we may admire the various bays and lakes, the inlets, promontories, and straits, the mountains and woodlands of this rare corner of creation — and, compared with it, we can boast of no scenery so beautiful — the Valley of Grand Pré transcends all the rest in the Province. Only our valley of Wyoming may match it, both in beauty and tradition. One has its Gertrude, the other its Evangeline. But Campbell never saw Wyoming. Longfellow never visited the Basin of Minas."

It is true the poet never visited the scene which his verse has made famous. It is said he feared his high ideal would become wrecked upon reality ; but he had no need ; he would have missed the forest primeval, but in all else the scene is in keeping with his fancy.

GRANDE FINALE.

"This is Acadia — this the land
 That weary souls have sighed for ;
This is Acadia, this the land
 Heroic hearts have died for ;
Yet, strange to tell, this promised land
 Has never been applied for!"

Thus says an old song, to which we must take exception in its final line. It has been, and is, applied for by an ever-increasing number of summer tourists who have found that here can the greatest amount of enjoyment and recreation be had at a moderate cost. The very idea of the old song explains the chief charm which the Provinces hold for summer sojourners from "The States." It is Acadia — fresh, rural, pastoral. The same conditions exist, among its rural types, as fifty years ago. Its very season is an oddity to the American guest, who may again enjoy the "garden truck," fruits and flowers of spring and early summer by a mid-summer trip to Acadia.

Phenomenally moderate — though not cheap in one sense of the word, — are all the accompaniments to thorough enjoyment of an outing passed beneath provincial skies. Hotel rates are low, and carriage hire does not deplete the pocket-book to an extent which renders that delightful pastime a thing to be indulged in sparingly. Good guides may be had in all hunting and fishing regions at "a dollar a day and found." Canoes and boats are plenty, while sail and steam are ready at every point of vantage to aid the tourist-traveller.

When these are coupled with cool, bracing air, clear skies, and delightful scenery, in a country colored by history and filled with the interest of tradition, song, and story, where every prospect is new and delightfully foreign to an American mind and fancy, it is not wonderful that the old song becomes inapplicable to one of the finest vacation regions extant.

Street in Grand Pré

Local Passenger Fares.

ONE WAY AND RETURN.

FROM BOSTON.

		ONE WAY.	RETURN.
Boston to	Annapolis, N. S., via St. John	$5.50	$9.75
"	Calais, Me.	4.50	8.00
"	Digby, N. S., via St. John	5.00	9.00
"	Eastport, Me.	4.00	7.50
"	Portland, Me.	1.00	2.00
"	Robbinston, Me.	4.50	8.00
"	St. Andrews, N. B.	4.50	8.00
"	St. John, N. B.	4.50	8.00

FROM PORTLAND.

		ONE WAY.	RETURN.
Portland to	Annapolis, N. S., via St. John	$5.50	$9.75
"	Calais, Me.	4.00	7.00
"	Digby, N. S.	5.00	9.00
"	Eastport, Me.	3.50	6.50
"	Robbinston, Me.	4.00	7.00
"	St. Andrews, N. B.	4.00	7.00
"	St. John, N. B.	4.00	7.00

FROM OTHER POINTS.

	ONE WAY.	RETURN.
Calais to St. John, N. B.	$1.50	$2.50
Robbinston to St. John, N. B.	1.50	2.50
St. Andrews to St. John, N. B.	1.50	2.50
Eastport to St. John, N. B.	1.50	2.25

☞ The above one-way rates are for limited tickets. Unlimited tickets are sold at an advance. Return tickets are good during the year in which they are purchased.

The same passenger rates will be in force during the time this Company runs six trips per week (see Summer Time-Table, first cover), via the Boston & Maine R.R. to Portland, thence by steamer, as by steamer direct; and tickets reading "by steamer" will be accepted via the Boston & Maine R.R. Also, tickets reading "via the R.R." to Portland, thence by steamer, will be accepted by direct steamer from Boston.

TARIFF OF RATES.

SUBJECT TO SLIGHT CHANGES WITHOUT NOTICE.

DESTINATION.	FROM BOSTON.		FROM PORTLAND.	
	UNLIMITED.	LIMITED.	UNLIMITED.	LIMITED.
AMHERST, N. S.	$8.25	....	$7.75	....
do. and Return	13.65	....	12.65	....
Andover, N. B.	8.80	....	8.30	....
do. and Return	14.45	....	13.45	....
Annapolis, N. S.	6.50	$5.50	6.50	$5.50
do. and Return	9.75	....	9.75	....
Antigonish, N. S.	10.75	10.25	10.25	9.75
do. and Return	17.40	....	16.40	....
Auburn, Me. (M. C. R.R.)	2.00	....	....	....
do. (G. T. R'y)	2.00	....	....	....
Augusta, Me.	3.00	....	....	....
Aylesford, N. S.	7.30	6.80	6.80	6.30
do. and Return	12.10	....	11.10	....
BADDECK, C. B.	13.50	13.00	13.00	12.50
do. and Return	22.60	....	21.60	....
Bath, Me.	2.25	....	....	....
Bathurst, N. B.	9.50	....	9.00	....
do. and Return	15.45	....	14.45	....
Beaver Bank	8.70	8.20	8.20	7.70
Berwick, N. S.	7.45	6.95	6.95	6.45
do. and Return	12.35	....	11.35	....
Bethel, Me.	3.65	....	....	....
Bethlehem, N. H.	5.55	....	....	....
Bridgetown, N. S.	6.50	6.00	6.00	5.50
do. and Return	11.00	....	10.00	....
Brunswick, Me.	2.00	....	....	....
CALAIS, Me.	5.50	4.50	5.00	4.00
do. and Return	8.00	....	7.00	....
Caledonia Corner, N. S.	9.00	8.00	8.50	7.50
Cambridge, N. S.	7.60	7.10	7.10	6.60
do. and Return	12.60	....	11.60	....
Campbellton, N. B.	10.50	....	10.00	....
do. and Return	17.00	....	16.00	....
Campobello, N. B.	5.25	4.25	4.75	3.75
do. and Return	8.00	....	7.00	....
Caribou, N. B. (via River and Rail)	9.50	....	9.00	....
do. and Return	15.50	....	14.50	....
Charlottetown, P. E. I.	9.50	....	9.00	....
do. and Return	16.25	....	15.25	....
Chatham, N. B.	9.00	....	8.50	....
do. and Return	14.75	....	13.75	....
Crawford House, N. H.	4.30	....	....	....
DALHOUSIE, N. B.	10.45	....	9.95	....
do. and Return	16.95	....	15.95	....
Digby, N. S.	6.00	5.00	6.00	5.00
do. and Return	9.00	....	9.00	....
Dorchester, N. B.	7.75	....	7.25	....
do. and Return	12.85	....	11.85	....
EASTPORT, Me.	5.00	4.00	4.50	3.50
do. and Return	7.50	....	6.50	....
Ellershouse, N. S.	8.80	8.00	8.30	7.50
do. and Return	14.65	....	13.65	....
FABYAN'S, N. H.	4.75	....	....	....
Falmouth, N. S.	8.25	7.75	7.75	7.25
do. and Return	14.00	....	13.00	....

TARIFF OF RATES.—Continued.

DESTINATION.	FROM BOSTON.		FROM PORTLAND.	
	UNLIMITED.	LIMITED.	UNLIMITED.	LIMITED.
Fort Fairfield, Me. (via River and Rail).	9.20	....	8.70	....
do. and Return	15.05	....	14.05	....
Fredericton, N. B. (via River)	5.50	....	5.00	....
do. and Return	9.50	....	8.50	....
GRAND PRE, N. S.	8.00	7.50	7.50	7.00
do. and Return	13.45	....	12.45	....
HALIFAX, N. S. (via I. C. R'y)	9.50	9.00	9.00	8.50
do. and Return	15.50	....	14.50	....
do. (via W. A. R'y)	9.80	8.20	9.30	7.70
do. and Return	15.50	....	14.50	....
Hantsport, N. S.	8.25	7.75	7.75	7.25
do. and Return	13.85	....	12.85	....
Har. Au Bouche	11.50	11.00	11.00	10.50
Harcourt, N. B.	8.05	....	7.35	....
do. and Return	13.30	....	12.30	....
Heatherton	11.10	10.60	10.60	10.10
Hopewell	9.50	9.00	9.00	8.50
Houlton, Me.	7.75	6.50	7.25	6.00
KENTVILLE, N. S.	7.75	7.25	7.25	6.75
do. and Return	13.00	....	12.00	....
Kingston, N. S.	7.05	6.55	6.55	6.05
do. and Return	11.75	....	10.75	....
LAWRENCETOWN, N. S.	6.70	6.20	6.20	5.70
do. and Return	11.25	....	10.25	....
Lewiston, Me.	2.00	....	....	....
Liverpool, N. S.	....	9.00	....	8.50
Londonderry, N. S.	9.25	9.00	8.75	8.50
do. and Return	15.10	....	14.10	....
MECHANIC FALLS, Me.	2.30	....	....	....
Metapedia, N. B.	10.70	....	10.20	....
do. and Return	17.35	....	16.35	....
Meteghan, N. S.	6.75	6.25	6.25	5.75
Middleton, N. S.	6.85	6.35	6.35	5.85
do. and Return	11.50	....	10.50	....
Moncton, N. B.	7.15	....	6.65	....
do. and Return	12.00	....	11.00	....
Montreal, P. Q. (G. T. R'y)	8.50	....	....	....
do. (via M. C. R'v)	8.50	....	....	....
Mt. Uniacke, N. S.	9.10	8.25	8.60	7.75
do. and Return	15.15	....	14.15	....
Mulgrave, N. S.	11.55	11.00	11.05	10.50
do. and Return	17.75	....	16.75	....
NEW CASTLE, N. B.	8.80	....	8.30	....
do. and Return	14.40	....	13.40	....
New Glasgow, N. S.	9.50	9.00	9.00	8.50
do. and Return	15.50	....	14.50	....
New Mills, N. B.	10.10	....	9.60	....
do. and Return	16.45	....	15.45	....
North Conway, N. H.	2.45	....	....	....
Norway, Me.	2.05	....	....	....
OLD ORCHARD, Me.	1.35	....	....	....
Oxford, N. S.	8.80	....	8.30	....
do. and Return	14.50	....	13.50	....
PARADISE, N. S.	6.60	6.10	6.10	5.60
do. and Return	11.10	....	10.10	....
Peticodiac, N. B.	6.50	....	6.00	....
do. and Return	11.00	....	10.00	....
Pictou, N. S.	9.50	9.00	9.00	8.50
do. and Return	15.50	....	14.50	....

TARIFF OF RATES.—Continued.

DESTINATION.	FROM BOSTON.		FROM PORTLAND.	
	UNLIMITED.	LIMITED.	UNLIMITED.	LIMITED.
Poland Springs.....................	$2.75	....	....	....
Portland, Me.....................	1.00	....	....	....
do. and Return........	2.00	....	....	....
do. and Return (Rail)...	4.00	$3.50	....	....
Port Williams, N. S...............	7.95	7.45	$7.45	$6.95
do. ....and Return.......	13.20	....	12.20	....
Presque Isle, Me. (via River and Rail)..	9.90	....	9.40	....
Profile House, N. H...............	6.55	....	....	....
do. and Return........	11.10	....	....	....
Pt. Du Chene, N. B................	....	7.50	....	7.00
do. and Return........	12.50	....	11.50	....
Pt. Hawkesbury, C. B..............	12.00	11.10	11.50	10.60
do. and Return........	17.00	....	16.90	....
Pt. Hastings.....................	12.05	11.15	11.55	10.65
do. and Return........	18.00	....	17.00	....
ROBBINSTON, Me................	5.50	4.50	5.00	4.00
do. and Return........	8.00	....	7.00	....
Round Hill, N. S...................	6.50	6.00	6.00	5.50
do. and Return........	11.00	....	10.00	....
SACKVILLE, N. B...............	....	8.10	....	7.60
do. and Return........	13.35	....	12.35	....
Salisbury, N. B....................	6.80	....	6.30	....
do. and Return........	11.40	....	10.40	....
Stewiacke, N. S....................	9.50	9.00	9.00	8.50
do. and Return........	15.50	....	14.50	....
Straits Canso, N. S. (Pt. Hawksbury)...	12.00	11.10	11.50	10.60
do. and Return........	17.90	....	16.90	....
Summerside, P. E. I................	....	8.25	....	7.75
do. and Return........	14.00	....	13.00	....
Sussex, N. B.....................	....	5.80	....	5.30
do. and Return........	10.00	....	9.00	....
Sydney, C. B. (all Rail)............	....	12.00	....	11.50
do. and Return........	18.75	....	17.75	....
THOMPSON, N. S...............	8.85	....	8.35	....
do. and Return........	14.50	....	13.50	....
Tracadie, N. S.....................	11.25	10.80	10.75	10.30
Truro, N. S........................	9.50	8.94	9.00	8.44
do. and Return........	15.50	....	14.50	....
WATERVILLE, N. S.............	7.50	7.00	7.00	6.50
do. and Return........	12.50	....	11.50	....
Wentworth, N. S...................	9.00	....	8.50	....
do. and Return........	14.80	....	13.80	....
Weymouth, N. S...................	6.80	5.80	6.30	5.30
Whycocomaugh, C. B..............	14.40	13.50	13.90	13.00
Wilmot, N. S.....................	6.95	6.45	6.45	5.95
do. and Return........	11.55	....	10.55	....
Windsor, N. S.....................	8.55	7.75	8.05	7.25
do. and Return........	14.00	....	13.00	....
Wolfville, N. S....................	8.00	7.50	7.50	7.00
do. and Return........	13.30	....	12.30	....
Woodstock, N. B. (via Calais)........	7.75	6.50	7.25	6.00
YARMOUTH, N. S...............	8.45	6.50	7.95	6.00
do. and Return........	12.75	....	11.75	....

For International S. S. Co.'s Local Rates See Page 89.

VIEW FROM INTERNATIONAL STEAMSHIP COMPANY'S DOCK, EASTPORT, ME.

MISCELLANEOUS TOURS.

Parties of ten or more travelling at one time will be furnished with special rates, upon application to the General Agent of the Company, Boston, Mass.

No 1.   **Annapolis and Return.** $9.75
Boston to St. John by International S. S. Co.; St. John to Annapolis by Bay of Fundy S. S. Co.; return same route.

No. 2.   **Antigonish, N. S., and Return.** $17.40
Boston to St. John by International S. S. Co.; St. John to Antigonish by Intercolonial R'y; return same route.

No. 3.   **Calais, Me., and Return.** $8.00
Boston to Eastport by International S. S. Co.; Eastport to Calais by Frontier S. B. Co.; return same route.

No. 4.   **Campobello, N. B., and Return.** $8.00
Boston to Eastport by International S. S. Co.; Eastport to Campobello by Campobello S. B. Co., return same route.

No. 5.   **Charlottetown, P. E. I., and Return.** $16.25
Boston to St. John by International S. S. Co.; St. John to Pt. Du Chene by Intercolonial R'y; Pt. Du Chene to Summerside by Charlottetown Steam Nav. Co.; Summerside to Charlottetown by P. E. I. R'y; return same route.

No. 6.   **Charlottetown, P. E. I., and Return.** $20.00
Boston to St. John by International S. S. Co.; St. John to Pt. Du Chene by Intercolonial R'y; Pt. Du Chene to Summerside by Charlottetown Steam Nav. Co.; Summerside to Charlottetown by P. E. I. R'y; Charlottetown to Picton by Charlottetown Steam Nav. Co.; Picton to Halifax by Intercolonial R'y; Halifax to Boston by Canada Atlantic S. S. Line.

No. 7.   **Digby, N. S., and Return.** $9.00
Boston to St. John by International S. S. Co.; St. John to Digby by Bay of Fundy S. S. Co.; return same route.

No. 8.   **Eastport, Me., and Return.** $7.50
Boston to Eastport by International S. S. Co.; Eastport to Boston by International S. S. Co.

No. 9.   **Fort Fairfield and Return.** $15.05
Boston to St. John by International S. S. Co.; St. John to Fredericton by Star Line Steamers; Fredericton to Ft. Fairfield by Canadian Pacific R'y; return same route.

No. 10.   **Halifax and Return.** $15.50
Boston to St. John by International S. S. Co.; St. John to Annapolis by Bay of Fundy S. S. Co.; Annapolis to Halifax by Windsor & Annapolis R'y; return same route.

No. 11.   **Halifax and Return.** $15.50
Boston to St. John by International S. S. Co.; St. John to Halifax by Intercolonial R'y; return same route.

No. 12.   **Halifax and Return.** $17.50
Boston to St. John by International S. S. Co.; St. John to Halifax by Intercolonial R'y; Halifax to Annapolis by Windsor & Annapolis R'y; Annapolis to St. John by Bay of Fundy S. S. Co.; St. John to Boston by International S. S. Co.; or vice versa.

No. 13.   **Halifax and Return.** $16.90
Boston to St. John by International S. S. Co.; St. John to Halifax by Intercolonial R'y; Halifax to Boston by Canada Atlantic S. S. Line.

No. 14.   **Kentville and Return.** $13.00
Boston to St. John by International S. S. Co.; St. John to Annapolis by Bay of Fundy S. S. Co.; Annapolis to Kentville by Windsor & Annapolis R'y; return same route.

No. 15.   **Montreal and Return.** $26.50
Boston to St. John by International S. S. Co.; St. John to Montreal by Intercolonial R'y; Montreal to Boston by Canadian Pacific R'y, via Newport.

No. 16.   **Montreal and Return.** $26.50
Boston to St. John by International S. S. Co.; St. John to Montreal by Canadian Pacific Short Line; Montreal to Boston by Canadian Pacific R'y via Newport.

No. 17.   **Mulgrave and Return.** $17.75
Boston to St. John by International S. S. Co.; St. John to Mulgrave by Intercolonial R'y; return same route.

No. 18.   **New Castle, N. B., and Return.** $14.40
Boston to St. John by International S. S. Co.; St. John to New Castle by Intercolonial R'y; return same route.

MISCELLANEOUS TOURS. — Continued.

No. 19.   **Pictou, N. S., and Return.** $15.50
Boston to St. John by International S. S. Co.; St. John to Truro by Intercolonial R'y; return same route.

No. 20.   **Portland, Me., and Return.** $2 00
Boston to Portland by International S. S. Co.; Portland to Boston by International S. S. Co.

No. 21.   **Portland, Me., and Return.** $4 00
Boston to Portland by International S. S Co.; Portland to Boston by Boston & Maine R.R.; if limited ticket, $3.50.

No. 22.   **Sydney, C. B., and Return.** $22.75
Boston to St. John by International S. S. Co.; St. John to Mulgrave by Intercolonial R'y; Mulgrave to Sydney by Bras d'Or Lake S. S.; return same route.

No. 23.   **Sydney, C. B., and Return.** $18.75
Boston to St. John by International S. S. Co.; St. John to Sydney by Intercolonial R'y; return same route.

No. 24.   **St. John and Return.** $12.50
Boston to St. John by International S. S. Co.; St. John to Boston, all rail.

No. 25.   **Summerside, P. E. I., and Return.** $14.00
Boston to St. John by International S. S. Co.; St. John to Pt. Du Chene by Intercolonial R'y; Pt. Du Chene to Summerside by Charlottetown Steam Nav. Co.; return same route.

No. 26.   **Truro, N. S , and Return.** $15.50
Boston to St. John by International S. S. Co.; St. John to Truro by Intercolonial R'y; return same route.

No. 27.   **Three Provinces Excursion.** $22.10
Boston to St. John by International S. S. Co ; St. John to Annapolis by Bay of Fundy S. S. Co.; Annapolis to Halifax by Windsor & Annapolis R'y; Halifax to Pictou by Intercolonial R'y; Pictou to Charlottetown by Charlottetown Steam Nav. Co.; Charlottetown to Summerside by P. E. I. R'y; Summerside to Pt. Du Chene by Charlottetown Steam Nav. Co.; Pt. Du Chene to St. John by Intercolonial R'y; St. John to Boston by International S. S. Co. This tour may be reversed, if desired, at same rate.

No. 28.   **Windsor and Return.** $14.00
Boston to St. John by International S. S. Co.; St. John to Annapolis by Bay of Fundy S. S. Co.; Annapolis to Windsor by Windsor & Annapolis R'y; return same route.

No. 29.   **Yarmouth, N. S., and Return.** $12.75
Boston to St. John by International S. S. Co.; St. John to Digby by Bay of Fundy S. S. Co.; Digby to Yarmouth by Western Counties R'y; return same route.

No. 30.   **Yarmouth, N. S., and Return.** $10.50
Boston to St. John by International S. S. Co.; St. John to Digby by Bay of Fundy S. S. Co.; Digby to Yarmouth by Western Counties R'y; Yarmouth to Boston by Yarmouth S. S. Co.

GENERAL INFORMATION TO PASSENGERS.

RETURN TICKETS are on sale to all principal points, and a large saving is made by purchasing the same. All return tickets entitle the passenger to stop-over privileges.

STATEROOMS AND MEALS. — Rooms may be engaged in advance upon application by letter or telegram to the local agents of the company. Stateroom berths are not sold by this company. Rooms are $1.00, $1.50 and $2 00 each. There are also several bridal and family rooms on each steamer, varying in price from $3.00 to $4.00. Meals are served on the American plan, at the following prices: Breakfast or supper, 50 cents; dinner, 75 cents.

CHILDREN'S TICKETS. — Children between the ages of five and twelve, half-fare; under five, free.

REDEMPTION OF TICKETS. — In the purchase of tickets, passengers are reminded that any portion of a ticket not used will be redeemed at its value at the Boston Wharf Agency, either by mail or upon personal application. This will apply to tickets issued by this company over its connections as well as over its own lines.

STEAMERS' LANDINGS. — From BOSTON, the steamers of the St. John line leave the *south side* of Commercial Wharf. AT PORTLAND, the steamers leave Railroad Wharf, foot of State Street. AT EASTPORT, the steamers of the International S. S. Co., the Campobello steamer, the St. Croix River steamer for St. Andrews, Robbinston and Calais, and steamer M. & M. for Pembroke, land at same pier. At ST. JOHN, the company's pier is at Reed's Point.

LUBEC.

SIXTEEN years before the Pilgrims landed on Plymouth Rock, the French found their way to Lubec and were the first settlers.

In 1758 French Acadians, escaping from Nova Scotia, settled along this coast.

Here is located the most eastern lighthouse on the United States coast, established in 1809.

During the past few years Lubec has made rapid strides as a favorite stopping-off place for tourists. There are several well-equipped hotels. The International Steamship Company are building a substantial wharf for the accommodation of the growing passenger and freight business.

NORTH LUBEC.

It is doubtful if any portion of the coast of Maine has grown so rapidly into popular favor as this charming neck of land.

It is the most eastern part of Uncle Sam's broad domain. The scenery is charming; the climate unsurpassed. As high an authority as General Greeley says, "It contains all the conditions essential to comfort and health during the heated term."

Men interested in the Young Men's Christian Associations in New England, in casting about for a choice location for a summer resort for their members and families, had their attention called to this place. They found that "the half had not been told" them.

Since the summer of 1889 encampments under moral and Christian influence have been held, under the control of representatives of the Young Men's Christian Associations of New England.

The variety of scenery, the romantic islands, the unexcelled opportunities for boating and fishing, together with the moral surroundings of this already popular neck of land, have placed it in the front ranks of seaside summer resorts.

The North Lubec Improvement Company own between six hundred and seven hundred acres of land, and their latest acquisition is one of the best springs in Maine. James F. Babcock, a chemical expert of Boston, has analyzed the water and pronounced it "exceedingly pure, as regards the presence of organic matter, and in its general character and composition resembles the Poland and other water of that class."

A spacious hotel, "The Ne-mat-ta-no," has been erected. All its appointments are first-class, and yet the rates are much lower than those charged at other seaside hotels. Families and young men who do not care for hotel life and desire to economize, can be accommodated at the neat farmhouses at about $5.00 per week. All who attend the encampment, whether located at the hotel or not, are considered a "member of the family." A casino for public meetings and entertainments, a gymnasium, a bowling alley, tennis courts and croquet grounds are among the pleasing features of the encampment. Next season there will be the best attractions of any previous season. Evangelist Geo. S. Avery will conduct evangelistic meetings and give a series of Bible readings during the month of July. Evangelist W. S. Martin, Chalktalker N. S. Greet, and others, will assist during August, and the excursions, fishing parties, and musical and literary entertainments will be all that can be desired.

CONNECTING LINES EAST OF BOSTON.

SPECIAL NOTICE.

The time-tables given below are substantially correct at the time this book goes to press. Changes, however, occur when the Summer Arrangements of the lines take effect, and passengers are respectfully referred to the official publications of the several lines, also to the Pathfinder Railway Guide, published at Boston, monthly, and to the Travelers' Official Railway Guide, published monthly at New York, which contain time-tables of all lines in the United States and Canada.

BOSTON & MAINE RAILROAD. — Trains leaving Boston at 12.30 P. M. (Eastern Division) and 1 P. M. (Western Division) connect with the steamers of the International Steamship Co. at Portland. Trains for Boston leave Portland (Western Division) at 6.30 and 8.40 A. M., 12.40 and 3.30 P. M., and (on the Eastern Division) at 2.10 and 8.45 A. M., 1.00 and 6.00 P. M.

WESTERN DIVISION LOCAL TRAINS, FROM PORTLAND

For Old Orchard Beach, Saco, Biddeford, and intermediate stations, 6.30, 8.40 and 10.25 A. M., 3.30 and 6.15 P. M. For Kennebunk, 6.30, 8.40 A. M., 12.45, 3.30 and 6.15 P. M. For Wells Beach, 6.30, 8.40 A. M., and 3.30 P. M. For North Berwick, Great Falls and Dover, 6.30, 8.40 A. M., 12.45 and 3.30 P. M. For Exeter, Haverhill, Lawrence and Lowell, 6.30, 8.40 A. M., and 3.30 P. M. For Rochester, Farmington, Alton Bay and Wolfboro', 8.40 A. M., 12.45 and 3.30 P. M. For Manchester and Concord (via Lawrence), 8.40 A. M. For Manchester and Concord (via Newmarket Junction), 6.30 A. M. and 3.30 P. M.

EASTERN DIVISION TRAINS

Leave Portland at 2.10 A. M. for Boston (night Pullman), stopping at Biddeford, Kittery, Portsmouth, Newburyport, Ipswich, Salem, Lynn, Chelsea and Somerville.
Leave Portland for Boston and important way stations at 9.00 A. M.
Leave Portland 1.00 P. M. for Boston, stopping at way-stations to Portsmouth.
Leave Portland 3.25 P. M. for Cape Elizabeth.
Leave Portland at 6 P. M. (express for Boston), stopping only at principal points.

BOOTHBAY, MOUSE AND SQUIRREL ISLANDS. — (Twenty-five miles.) Eastern Steamboat Co. Steamers leave Bath, Me., daily (except Sunday), after arrival of noon trains of Maine Central Railroad from Portland.

CONNECTING LINES EAST OF BOSTON. — Continued.

BAY OF FUNDY STEAMSHIP CO. — (Sixty miles.) (St. John, Digby, and Annapolis, Nova Scotia Line.) Steamers, during July and August, leave St. John every day (except Sunday) at 7.30 A. M., local St. John time, for Digby and Annapolis, N. S., connecting at these points for all parts of Western Nova Scotia. Returning, leave Annapolis and Digby same afternoon, arriving at St. John about 7.00 P. M. For other time tables, see Company's circulars and daily papers.

BAY DE CHALEUR, N. B. — Steamer "Admiral" leaves Dalhousie (north shore of N. B.) every Wednesday and Saturday morning for Gaspe, N. B., calling at intermediate ports. Returning, leaves Gaspe Monday and Thursday mornings.

CAMPOBELLO STEAMBOAT CO. — (One and one half miles.) Steamers of the various Ferry companies for the Island of Campobello leave Eastport at frequent intervals during the day.

CAPE BRETON STEAMER LINE. — (Eighty miles.) (Bras d'Or Lake Steam Navigation Co.) After commencement of the summer time-table of the Intercolonial Railway, steamers leave Mulgrave every Tuesday, Thursday, and Saturday, on arrival of express train from St. John, for Sydney, passing through Lennox Passage and St. Peter's Canal, for Grand Narrows, Baddeck and Bouiarderie Islands in Bras d'Or Lakes. Returning, leave Sydney (calling at above places) Mondays, Wednesdays and Fridays, for Mulgrave, connecting with express for St. John and all points west.

FRONTIER STEAMBOAT CO. — (Thirty miles.) (Eastport, St. Andrews, Robbinston, Calais — opp. St. Stephen) Steamer "Rose Standish" runs in regular connection with the steamers of the International Steamship Co. to and from Eastport, performing a daily service on the St. Croix River.

GRAND TRUNK RAILWAY. — For Auburn and Lewiston, 7.20, 9.00 A. M., 12.45 and 5.12 P. M. For Gorham, N. H., 9.00 A. M., 1.30 and 5.12 P. M. For Montreal and Chicago, 9.00 A. M. and 1.30 P. M. For Quebec, 1.30 P. M. For Buckfield and Canton, 9.00 A. M. and 1.30 P. M.

SHORE LINE RAILWAY. — (Between St. John, St. George and St. Stephen, N. B.) Trains leave Carleton (ferry from St. John) daily (Sundays excepted) at 7.45 A. M.

GLEN HOUSE STAGE LINE. — Stages leave Glen Station, Maine Central Railroad (White Mountains Division), on arrival of train from Portland, 11.00 A. M., train from Boston, 2.00 P. M.; also leave Gorham, N. H., (Grand Trunk Railway) on arrival of train leaving Portland at 9.00 A. M. and 1.30 P. M.; leave the summit of Mount Washington for Glen House at 7.00 A. M. and 2.00 P. M.

INTERCOLONIAL RAILWAY. — Trains of this road leave St. John morning and evening for Moncton, Campbellton, Amherst, Truro, Halifax, and all important stations on main line both north and south of Moncton. For hours of leaving, see official time-cards.

LUBEC AND EASTPORT FERRY. — (Three miles.) Ferry steamers leave Eastport for Lubec at frequent intervals day and evening.

CONNECTING LINES EAST OF BOSTON.—Continued.

LUBEC AND MACHIAS STAGE.—(Twenty-eight miles.) Leaves Lubec daily for Machias. Returning, leaves Machias daily for Lubec.

MAINE CENTRAL RAILWAY.— Trains leave Portland as follows on and after June 27th, 1892:

For Auburn and Lewiston, 8.30 A. M., 1.15 and 5.10 P. M. Lewiston, via Brunswick, 6.40 A. M., 1.00, 1.20, 5.05 and ‡11.30 P. M. For Bath, 6.40 A. M., 1.00, 1.20, 5.05 and ‡11.30 P. M. Rockland and Knox & Lincoln Railroad, 6.40 A. M. and 1.20 and ‡11.30 P. M. Brunswick, Gardiner, Hallowell and Augusta, 6.40 A. M., 1.00, 1.20, 5.05 and ‡11.20 P. M. Farmington, via Lewiston, 8.30 A. M. and 1.15 P. M.; via Brunswick, 1.20 P. M. Monmouth, Winthrop, Lake Maranacook, Readfield, Oakland and North Anson, 1.15 P. M. Waterville and Skowhegan, via Lewiston, 1.15 P. M., and Waterville only at 5.10 P. M.; via Augusta, 6.40 A. M., 1.00, 1.20 and ‡11.30 P. M. Belfast and Dexter, 1.15, 1.20, ‡11.30 P. M. Bangor, via Lewiston, 1.15 P. M.; via Augusta, 6.40 A. M., 1.00, 1.20, ‡11.30 P. M. Bangor and Piscataquis Railroad, via Dexter, 6.40 A. M. and 1.00 P. M.; via Oldtown, 6.40 A. M. ‡11.30 P. M. Ellsworth and Bar Harbor, 1.00, 1.20, ‡11.30 P. M. Vanceboro', St. Stephen (Calais), Aroostook County, St. John, Halifax, and the Provinces, 1.15, 1.20, ‡11.30 P. M.

‡Night express, with sleeping-car attached, runs every night, Sundays included, through to Lewiston (via Brunswick), Bath, Rockland, and Bangor, but not to Skowhegan Monday mornings, or to Belfast and Dexter, or beyond Bangor, excepting to Bar Harbor, Sunday mornings.

WHITE MOUNTAINS LINE.—For Cumberland Mills, 8.45 A. M., 1.05, 6.15 P. M. For Sebago Lake, 8.45 A. M., 1.05 and 6.15 P. M. For Bridgton, 8.45 A. M., 1.05 and 6.15 P. M. Fryeburg, North Conway, Glen Station, Crawford's, and Fabyan's and Montreal, 8.45 A. M. and 6.15 P. M. Jefferson and Lancaster, 8.45 A. M. and 1.05 P. M. Colebrook and Quebec, 1.05 P. M.

NOVA SCOTIA CENTRAL RAILWAY.— Trains of this railway connect at Middleton (W. & A. R'y) for New Germany, Lunenburg, Bridgewater, Malone Bay, and other points on South Shore, including Liverpool.

CANADIAN PACIFIC RAILWAY.— (St. John to Fredericton, Grand Falls, Vanceboro', St. Stephen, St. Andrews, etc.) Trains leave St. John for Fredericton, St. Stephen, St. Andrews, Houlton, Bangor, etc., at 6.10 and 8.55 A. M. For Fredericton at 4.45 P. M. For St. Stephen, St. Andrews, Houlton, Bangor, etc., at 8.30 P. M.

PORTLAND AND NEW YORK LINE.—(Three hundred and forty miles.) (Maine Steamship Co.) Steamers leave Portland for New York, calling at Martha's Vineyard, every Monday, Wednesday and Saturday at 6 P. M. Returning, leave New York every Monday, Wednesday and Saturday at 5 P. M.

PORTLAND AND BOOTHBAY LINE.—Steamer leaves Portland Tuesdays and Saturdays at 8.00 A. M., for Squirrel Island, Boothbay, Heron Island, South Bristol, and East Boothbay, and for Pemaquid every Thursday at 8.00 A. M. Returning, leaves Boothbay every Monday and Thursday at 8.00 A. M. for Portland and intermediate points. Also leaves Pemaquid for Portland Fridays at 7.00 A. M.

CONNECTING LINES EAST OF BOSTON. — Continued.

MT. DESERT AND MACHIAS LINE. — After June 27th a new steamer, the "Frank Jones," will make tri-weekly round trips between Rockland, Bar Harbor and Machiasport, leaving Rockland Tuesdays, Thursdays and Saturdays at 6.00 A. M., and returning from Machiasport, Mondays, Wednesdays and Fridays.

PORTLAND & ROCHESTER RAILROAD. — Trains leave Portland as follows: — For Worcester, Clinton, Ayer Junction, Nashua, Windham and Epping at 7.30 A. M. and 12.30 P. M. For Manchester, Concord, and points north at 7.30 A. M. and 12.30 P. M. For Rochester, Springvale, Alfred, Waterboro' and Saco River at 7.30 A. M., 12.30 and 5.30 P. M. For Gorham at 7.30 and 10.00 A. M., 12.30, 3.00, 5.30, 6.20 and 11.15 P. M. For Westbrook (Saccarappa), Cumberland Mills, Westbrook Junction and Woodford's at 7.30 and 10.00 A. M., 12.30, 3.00, 5.30, 6.20 and 11.15 P. M.

PORTLAND AND BOSTON STEAMERS. — (One hundred and ten miles.) (Portland Steam Packet Co.) Leave Portland at 7.00 P. M. daily. Returning, leave Boston at 7.00 P. M. daily. In summer, special Sunday-evening trips are made in both directions.

PEMBROKE AND EASTPORT LINE. — Steamer M. & M. runs regularly between Pembroke and Eastport, making close connections at the latter place with International Steamers.

CHARLOTTETOWN STEAM NAVIGATION CO. — Steamer leaves Point du Chene about 2.00 P.M. daily, except Sundays, for Summerside. Returning, leaves Summerside about 8.00 A.M. Leaves Pictou, Monday, Wednesday, Friday and Saturday, about 1.00 P.M. for Charlottetown. Returning, leaves Charlottetown, Monday, Wednesday, Thursday and Saturday about 7.00 A.M.

STAR LINE STEAMER leaves Indiantown at 9.00 A.M. week-days. Returning, leaves Fredericton 8.00 A.M. week-days.

WINDSOR & ANNAPOLIS RAILWAY. — Trains leave Annapolis as follows: — 6.10 A.M. and 1.40 P.M. daily (except Sunday), for all points between Annapolis and Halifax.

YARMOUTH & ANNAPOLIS RAILWAY. — (Between Digby and Yarmouth, N.S.) Leave Yarmouth, express daily at 8.00 A.M., arrive at Annapolis at 12.00 noon; Passenger and Freight Monday, Wednesday and Friday at 1.00 P.M., arrive at Annapolis 5.48 P.M. Leave Annapolis, express daily at 1.20 P.M., arrive at Yarmouth 5.20 P.M.; Passenger and Freight Tuesday, Thursday and Saturday at 7.30 A.M., arrive at Yarmouth 12.35 P.M.

CONNECTING LINES TO PORTLAND
AND SOUTH AND WEST FROM BOSTON.

THROUGH TRAINS—SUBJECT TO CHANGE.

Boston & Maine Railroad — Eastern Division.
  For PORTLAND — 7.30 and 6.15 A. M., 12.30 and 7.00 P. M.
  " WHITE MOUNTAINS — 7.30 A. M., 12.30 P. M.

Boston & Maine Railroad — Western Division.
  For PORTLAND — 7.30 and 8.30 A. M., 1.00 and 3.45 P. M.

} Morning trains and the 12.30 and 7.00 P. M. trains connect at Portland with steamers.
‡ No transfer.

Boston & Maine Railroad — Lowell Division.
  For MONTREAL, P. Q. — via Central Vermont Railroad — 8.30 A. M., 1.00 and 7.00 P. M.
  " — via Canadian Pacific Railway — 9.00 A. M., 8.00 P. M.
  " WHITE MOUNTAINS — 9.00 A. M.

Boston & Maine Railroad — Central Mass. Division.
  For HUDSON, WARE and NORTHAMPTON — 7.45 A. M., 4.30 P. M.

Boston & Albany Railroad.
  For NEW YORK — 5.00, 9.00 and 11.00 A. M., 4.00 and 11.00 P. M.
  " ALBANY — 5.00, 8.30 and 11.00 A. M., 3.00, 7.00 and 10.30 P. M.
  " THE WEST — 8.30 A. M., 3.00 and 7.02 P. M.

Fitchburg Railroad — Hoosac Tunnel Route.
  For MONTREAL, P. Q. — via Central Vermont Railroad — 8.00 and 11.30 A. M.
  " TROY, N. Y. — 6.30, 8.30 and 11.30 A. M., 3.00, 7.00 and 11.00 P. M.
  " THE WEST — 8.30 and 11.30 A. M., 3.00 and 7.00 P. M.

New York & New England Railroad.
  For NEW YORK — 8.30 A. M., 12.00 noon, 1.00 and 5.30 P. M.
  " PHILADELPHIA, BALTIMORE and WASHINGTON — 6.00 P. M.
  " NEW YORK — via Sound Steamer — 6.00 P. M.

Old Colony Railroad.
  For NEW YORK — via Fall River Line — 6.00 P. M.
  "   "   " — via Shore Line; all rail — 11.30 A. M., 1.00, 5.00 and 11.30 P. M.
  "   "   " — via Providence Line — Opens in June, 6.30 P. M.
  "   "   " — via Stonington Line — 6.30 P. M.

BOSTON AND PORTLAND BY DAYLIGHT.

RATES.	One Way.	Return.
Boston to Portland, Me.	$1.00	$2.00
" Auburn, Me.	2.00	....
" Augusta, Me.	3.00	....
" Bath, Me.	2.75	....
" Belfast, Me.	5.00	....
" Brunswick, Me.	2.00	....
" Crawford House, N. H.	4.30	6.85
" Fabyan's, N. H.	4.55	7.10
" Farmington, Me.	3.75	7.30
" Glen House, N. H. ....(via P. & O.)	6.05	10.00
" Gorham, N. H.	4.45	7.00
" Gardiner, Me.	2.75	....
" Hallowell, Me.	2.65	....
" Lewiston, Me.	2.00	....
" Montreal, P. Q. ....(via P. & O. R. R.)	8.50	14.50
" Montreal, P. Q. ....via G. T. R'y.)	8.50	14.50
" North Conway, N. H.	3.05	5.60
" Old Orchard, N. H.	1.35	2.50
" Poland Springs, Me.	2.75	5.00
" Skowhegan, Me.	4.50	....
" Waterville, Me.	3.75	....

STAGE CONNECTIONS.

At SHUBENACADIE with Stages daily for Maitland, Gay's River and Musquodoboit, and on Saturdays for Kennetcook and Noel.

At HOPEWELL with McDaniel's Stage Line for Springville, Bridgeville, St. Paul, Upper and Lower Caledonia, Smithfield and Melrose.

At TRURO, daily, with Stages for Clifton, Black Rock and Maitland, and tri-weekly for Earltown, and W. Branch River John.

At LONDONDERRY with Stages for Acadia Iron Mines, Great Village, Economy and Five Islands.

At SHEDIAC with Stages to and from Cocagne and Buctouche.

At HARCOURT with Stages for Richibucto, Kingston and other places on North Shore.

At NEWCASTLE with tri-weekly Stage for Red Bank, Whitneyville, Derby, Blissfield, Doaktown and Fredericton.

At CAMPBELLTON (during the winter) with Stage Line daily for Gaspe and Intermediate places on Baie de Chaleur.

At RIVIERE DU LOUP with Turner's Mail Line for Madawaska, N. B.

CAPE BRETON CONNECTIONS, 1893.

Intercolonial trains run through from Mulgrave to Grand Narrows and Sydney.

Steamship Marion will leave Sydney on Mondays, Wednesdays and Fridays, calling at Bouloidarie, Baddeck, Grand Narrows, St. Peters and Grandique Ferry, connecting with No. 20 Train. Returning, leave Mulgrave on arrival of No. 19 Train, for Sydney, calling at above points and connecting with Steamship Magnolia at Baddeck for Whycocomaugh, Little Narrows and Little Bras d'Or.

Steamship Neptune will leave Mulgrave on Mondays, Wednesdays and Fridays, on arrival of No. 19 Train, for East Bay, calling at Grandique Ferry and St. Peters. Returning from East Bay on Mondays, Wednesdays and Fridays in time to connect with No. 20 Train.

Steamship Ramouski will leave Mulgrave every Monday and Friday, on arrival of No. 19 Train, for Arichat and Canso; Tuesdays and Thursdays for Port Hood; Wednesdays and Saturdays for Guysboro. Returning from above points following mornings, so as to connect with No. 20 Train.

LIST OF HOTELS.

☞ This Company not responsible for errors or omissions.

City or Town.	Name of Hotel.	Proprietor.	Rooms	Rate Per Day	Rate Per Week
Amherst, N. S.	Terrace Hotel	N. C. Calhoun	40	$1.50	Special
	Amherst Hotel	Geo. McFarlane	75	1.00	"
Annapolis, N. S.	Clifton House	Wm. McLelland	34	1.50	$5.00 to $7.00
	American House	Mrs. J. H. McLeod	25	1.50	5.00 to 7.00
	Commercial House	Mrs. J. H. Salter	22	1.50	4.00 to 6.00
Aylesford, N. S.	Aylesford House	M. N. Graves	17	1.00	4.00
		Mrs. Corban	6	1.00	3.50
Berwick, N. S.	French Villa	Mrs. Vaughan	12	1.00	4.00
Bridgetown, N. S.	Grand Central	W. I. Glencross	22	1.50	Special
	Revere House	Mrs. Russell	12	1.50	"
Calais, Me.	Border City Hotel	D. M. Gardner	40	2.00	"
	St. Croix Exchange	J. K. Duran	50	2.00	"
	American House	J. G. Hamilton	40	2.00	"
Campobello, N. B.	Fy'n-y-Coed	Write Manager			
Cutler, Me.	Hotel Cutler	Write Eben Dean, 70 Devonshire Street, Boston.			
Dalhousie, N. B.	Inch Arran House			2.50 to 4.00	Special.
	Murphy's Hotel	Thos. Murphy		1.50	9.00
Digby, N. S.	Myrtle House	J. C. Morrison	25	2.00	7.00 to 10.00
	Royal Hotel	J. Daley	30	1.50	5.00 to 7.00
	Short's Hotel	Mrs. M. Short	20	1.50	5.00 to 7.00
	Burnham House	Mrs. J. Burnham	18	1.50	5.00 to 7.00
	Digby Hotel	Miss Smith	15	1.50	5.00 to 7.00
Eastport, Me.	Quoddy House	Kenney & Bucknam	100	2.00 to 3.00	Special.
Fredericton, N. B.	Barker House	F. B. Coleman	50	2.00 to 2.50	10.00 to 14.00
	Queen Hotel	J. A. Edwards	50	2.00 to 2.50	10.00 to 11.00
Halifax, N. S.	Queen Hotel	A. B. Sheraton	130	2.00 to 3.00	10.50 to 16.00
	Halifax Hotel	H. Hesslein	200	2.50 to 4.00	10.00 to 15.00
Kentville, N. S.	Lyons' Hotel	D. McLeod	18	1.50	Special.
	Kentville House	Jas. Lyons	20	1.50	"
	Porter House	Rufus Porter	38	1.25	5.00
	Revere House	Mrs. W. Redden	22	1.00	5.00
	American House	J. McIntosh	16	1.25	5.00
	Victoria Hotel	C. E. Farren	17	1.25	5.00
Kingston, N. S.	Kingston House	R. E. Davidson	18	1.00	5.00
Lawrencet'n, N. S.	Elm House	A. P. Phinney	8	1.25	4.00
	Valley House	N. H. Phinney	8	1.00	3.50
Middleton, N. S.	American House	D. Feindal	23	1.50	5.00 and 6.00
Moncton, N. B.	Brunswick House	Geo. McSweeney	50	2.00 to 3.00	Special.
	Commercial House		30	1.50 to 2.00	"
New Glasgow, N. S.	Vendome	D. McDearmid		Special.	
Pt. Hastings, C. B.	Caledonia Hotel		25	1.00	4.00 to 5.00
Portland, Me.	Falmouth Hotel	J. K. Martin	250	3.00 to 4.00	15.00 and up.
	United States	Foss & O'Connor	150	2.00 to 2.50	10.00 and up.
	Preble House	M. S. Gibson	118	2.50 to 3.00	Special.
	City Hotel	V. H. Sweet	80	2.00 to 2.50	"
	St. Julian Hotel	W. R. Underwood	50	1.00 to 3.00	"
St. Andrews, N. B.	Algonquin	Albert Miller	200	3.00 to 5.00	15.00 and up.
St. John, N. B.	Dufferin	F. A. Jones	50	3.00	Special.
	Victoria	D. W. McCormick	68	2.00 to 2.50	"
	Royal	Thos. F. Raymond	76	3.00	"
	New Victoria	J. L. McCloskey	50	2.00	"
	Belmont	John Sime			5.00
	Queen	J. C. Rickie	33	3.00	6.00
Summerside, P. E. I.	Clifton House	E. Mawley	29	1.50	Special.
	Hotel Russ	J. B. Russ	20	2.00	
Truro, N. S.	Pr. of Wales Hotel	Mrs. A. L. McKenzie	25	1.50	7.00
	Victoria Hotel	N. A. Ross	45	1.50	7.00
	Bigelow House	E. C. Bigelow	22	1.50	7.00
	Learment Hotel	A. H. Learment	30	1.50	Special.
Waterville, N. S.		W. H. Risteen	20	1.50	"
		T. A. Margeson	11	1.00	"
Weymouth, N. S.		Forbes Jones	8	1.00	
Windsor, N. S.	Avon House	John Cox	14	1.50	5.00 to 7.00
	Victoria Hotel	Thos. Doran		1.50	Special.
	Clifton House	F. Kelcup		1.50	"
	Somerset House	W. Gibson		1.00	"
	Windsor House	Thos. Gibson		1.25	"
Wolfville, N. S.	Acadia House	J. L. Franklyn	20	1.50	6.00
	Central Hotel	Mrs. C. R. Quin	18	1.50	Special.
	Wolfville House	H. D. Farrell	14	1.50	6.00
	Kent Lodge	Mrs. Haliburton	12	1.25	Special.
	American House	J. W. Harris	24	1.25	5.00
	Village Hotel	Mrs. Newcombe	14	1.25	5.00

www.ingramcontent.com/pod-product-compliance
Lightning Source LLC
Chambersburg PA
CBHW021919180426
43199CB00032B/946